Aid to Africa

Paul Streeten

Published by Praeger Publishers, Inc.

with the cooperation of the United Nations

The Praeger Special Studies program—utilizing the most modern and efficient book production techniques and a selective worldwide distribution network—makes available to the academic, government, and business communities significant, timely research in U.S. and international economic, social, and political development.

Aid to Africa
A Policy Outline
for the 1970's

PRAEGER SPECIAL STUDIES IN INTERNATIONAL ECONOMICS AND DEVELOPMENT

Praeger Publishers   New York   Washington   London

PRAEGER PUBLISHERS
111 Fourth Avenue, New York, N.Y. 10003, U.S.A.
5, Cromwell Place, London S.W.7, England

Published in the United States of America in 1972
by Praeger Publishers, Inc.

Library of Congress Catalog Card Number: 74-180854

Printed in the United States of America

The United Nations Economic Commission for Africa
(ECA) adopted at its eight session Resolution 169
(VIII) on the mobilization of external resources for
African development. It recommends the creation of
a Special Fund for African Development, requests the
Executive Secretary of the ECA inter alia to coordinate
closely his action in its implementation with that
of the President of the African Development Bank
(ADB) in mobilizing a special fund for the Bank.

This study of aid to Africa, which has been
undertaken by Professor Paul Streeten of Oxford
University, acting as a special service consultant
to the ECA, represents the first step toward implem-
enting resolution 169(VIII). Its objectives are
threefold. First, it gives an assessment both of
the volume and of the quality of the recent and current flow of external financial and technical resources
from official sources to Africa. Second, it provides,
on the basis of critical evaluation of donors' current policies and attitudes, a much-needed briefing
and a message to donors on the special needs of Africa
in the area of aid and international cooperation.
Third, the study establishes a case, in support of
meeting those special needs, for a growing contribution of soft resources, in particular for the
creation of an African Development Fund which donor
countries are expected to support.

Concerning the coordination of action between
the ECA and the ADB called for by resolution 169(VIII),
working contacts have already been established and
an interagency meeting comprising the two organizations
as well as the World Bank has been held. In addition
to agreement on the follow-up action to be taken
toward the establishment of the African Development
Fund, the initiative for which would continue to be
taken by the ADB, the participants in the interagency
meeting also discussed with the author, the contents

of this study. The study has thus benefited from
various views and suggestions expressed at that
meeting.

This study was submitted, together with the
report of the interagency meeting, to the tenth
session of the Council of Ministers of the ECA at
Tunis in February, 1971, for its consideration and
in order that directives for further action might be
established. It was also put before the fifth joint
meeting of the ECA/OAU Working Party on Trade and
Development in August, 1970, as a background document.

For publication in book form, tables were updated
to incorporate statistical data available as of August,
1971.

CONTENTS

LIST OF TABLES

xi

LIST OF CHARTS

LIST OF ABBREVIATIONS

ADB   African Development Bank

AID   Agency for International Development

DAC   Development Assistance Committee

ECA   Economic Commission for Africa

EDF   European Development Fund

EEC   European Economic Community

EIB   European Investment Bank

GNP   Gross National Product

IBRD   International Bank for Reconstruction and Development

IDA   International Development Association

IMF   International Monetary Fund

LDC   Less Developed Country

NNI   Net National Income

OECD   Organization for Economic Cooperation and Development

SDR   Special Drawing Right

UNCTAD United Nations Commission on Trade and Development

UNDP   United Nations Development Program

The purpose of this study* is to carry the
international discussion, which the Pearson Report
has aroused, a stage further. The intention is to
focus the light that Pearson has cast on the broad
area of development aid more sharply in three directions. One is geographical. Latin America and Asia
have had their highly articulate spokesmen and have
established schemes covering their whole regions,
such as the Colombo Plan and the Alliance for Progress. The voice of Africa has been comparatively
still, and there have been no cooperative projects
covering the whole continent. Yet, without in any
way detracting from the claims of other regions,
Africans have special claims of their own and special
reasons to plead for particular forms of more effective
international cooperation. This study attempts to
make a contribution to the articulation of these
claims.

The second focus is upon the concrete objectives
that lie behind the aggregate targets. Much of the
post-Pearson discussion has been, rightly, conducted
in terms of large aggregates of gross national products, savings, investment, and their growth rates.
Many differences and divergencies can be concealed
by such aggregations. Of course, these targets are
essential to sketch the outlines of the problem and
to harness political will. But in order to eradicate
the roots of poverty and in order to win the support
of those who believe that aid has in the past been
wasted, one must point to actually or potentially
successful applications of aid. The approach by
targets should be supplemented by an approach which
starts, as it were, at the other end. What, precisely,

---

*I am indebted to Akbar Noman for considerable
help in the preparation of this study.

do we wish to achieve? What are the main needs?
What are our priorities? How can we cooperate in
achieving them? What can developed countries contribute to this achievement? In this way effective
international cooperation can be given concrete
content and problems can be tackled at their roots.

The principal objectives underlying the recommendations of this study are (1) effective regional
and subregional cooperation in investment, production,
and trade; (2) not only accelerated growth rates of
average income but also its more equal distribution
and more jobs for the rapidly growing labor force;
and (3) more effective preparation, execution, and
management of projects that fit into these basic
development objectives.

Third, the discussion of this study is confined
to official external assistance. Private foreign
investment is excluded. Also excluded are trade,
international migration, and international monetary
issues, except where they have a direct bearing on
external assistance.

Such exclusions inevitably distort the picture.
Just as development is a complex system of interrelated
actions and responses on many fronts, so numerous
policies of advanced industrial countries have reper-
cussions that affect the development prospects of the
developing countries. To look at one set of policies
in isolation can therefore be highly misleading. It
is possible to undo the good done through external
assistance by measures in the field of trade or
migration or monetary arrangements. Devaluations
of major currencies, entry into the European Economic
Community (EEC) without adequate safeguards, and a
technological advance in a synthetic product that
knocks out the exports of a developing country might
serve as illustrations.

In spite of these difficulties, this study
confines itself to questions of official external
assistance. But the limitation should always be borne
in mind. The basic philosophy underlying it is the
now widely accepted view that external assistance

must be seen and judged in the context of international
cooperation for development. Development requires a
concerted effort over a wide range of policies of
developing as well as developed countries. In particular, the problem-oriented approach adopted in this
study presupposes that it is in the common interest
of all members of the world community to solve
certain problems jointly--improved nutrition; more,
and more efficient, jobs; improved schooling; rural
and industrial development; etc.--and that success
in this joint operation depends on all partners
contributing to the best of their ability. It is in
this context that expressions like "aid" or "official
external assistance" should be interpreted in the
following pages.

Aid to Africa

1

DONORS'
POLICIES

Donors' objectives, motives, and criteria in
giving aid are mixed; and the particular mixture
varies from one donor to another. One of the main
reasons for the disappointment with the aid policies
of the 1950's and 1960's must be sought in this fusion
and confusion of sometimes contradictory aims and
motives. This confusion also partly explains the
difficulties of effective coordination of donors'
policies. It is therefore useful to begin with a
brief summary of the main donors' contributions. A
serious difficulty in attempting to assess aid policies
is the fact that two of the three major European
donors were great colonial powers. Much of the aid
of Britian and France goes to countries whose educated
people were brought up in the same traditions, speak
the same language, and went to the same universities
as the members of the metropolitan country and have
in their own countries adopted similar ideas and
institutions. External assistance in these circumstances is just one strand in a complex of relationships. It is sometimes difficult to say where the
influence of aid ends and where the colonial legacy
begins.

FRENCH AID

French aid to traditionally foreign countries,
that is, countries that have not been under recent

3

TABLE 1

French Official Bilateral Aid Flows, 1962-67

	1962			1963			1964			
	From France (million $)	Total DAC Countries (million $)	Per-cent	From France (million $)	Total DAC Countries (million $)	Per-cent	From France (million $)	Total DAC Countries (million $)	Per-cent	From France (million $)
French Franc Area South of Sahara	325.9	359.1	90.8	337.3	386.8	87.2	345.6	405.6	85.2	321.0
French Overseas Territories[1]	37.8	37.8	100.0	43.3	43.3	100.0	68.6	68.6	100.0	61.3
Algeria	357.6	396.3	90.2	239.4	279.4	85.7	182.4	226.4	80.6	135.1
Morocco, Tunisia	45.4	148.7	30.5	71.7	175.3	40.9	79.9	167.3	47.8	60.5
Total Franc Zone	728.9	904.1	80.6	648.4	841.5	77.1	607.9	799.3	76.1	516.6
Cambodia, Laos, Vietnam	8.1	196.0	4.1	8.0	244.7	3.3	9.1	245.2	3.7	16.0
Total	737.0	1100.1	67.0	656.4	1086.2	60.4	617.0	1044.5	59.1	532.6
Other[2]	123.8	4252.9	2.9	165.0	4545.1	3.6	193.4	4347.7	4.5	191.9
Total Official Bilateral Aid	860.0	5353.0	16.1	821.4	5631.3	14.6	810.4	5392.2	15.0	724.5

	1965 Total DAC Countries (million $)	1965 Per-cent	1966 From France (million $)	1966 Total DAC Countries (million $)	1966 Per-cent	1967 From France (million $)	1967 Total DAC Countries (million $)	1967 Per-cent
French Franc Area South of Sahara	363.0	88.4	327.6	382.7	85.6	381.4	435.7	87.6
French Overseas Territories[1]	61.3	99.9	88.3	88.3	100.0	98.2	98.2	100.0
Algeria	144.0	93.8	97.7	121.1	80.7	92.0	107.5	85.6
Morocco, Tunisia	191.0	31.7	45.7	145.3	31.5	23.8	161.9	14.7
Total Franc Zone	698.0	79.6	471.0	649.1	72.7	497.2	705.1	70.5
Cambodia, Laos, Vietnam	389.4	4.1	16.3	589.2	2.8	19.2	542.0	3.5
Total	1087.4	49.0	487.3	1238.3	39.0	516.4	1247.1	41.0
Other[2]	4681.6	4.1	228.9	4728.1	4.8	270.8	4980.2	5.4
Total Official Bilateral Aid	5769.0	12.5	716.2	5966.4	12.0	787.2	6227.3	12.6

1. Including Reunion, a French overseas dept.
2. Includes Flows to French overseas territories and departments in Latin America and Oceania.

Source: OECD, Geographical Distribution of Financial Flows 1960-64, 1964, 1966-67.

French rule, was only about 12.5 percent of total
French net aid in 1967, although the share has been
growing over time. Most of this aid was in the form
of technical assistance. The objective is cultural
and economic and has been described in a French
publication as the defense of "cultural and economic
positions in a rapidly changing world by maintaining
an original form of contact and activities in developing countries."[1] The chief means is establishing
or strengthening the teaching of French. The influence of French aid in the traditionally foreign
countries has therefore probably been very slight
because it is small and the teaching of French is
likely to have only a delayed and very indirect effect
on development policy. Tables 1 and 2 show the
geographical distribution of French aid.

French policy toward her former colonies was
dominated by the concept of interdependence. The
Plan for the Economic and Social Development of the
French Union was designed to ensure the harmonious
development of the whole, not the self-sufficiency
of the parts. Aid consisted of a high proportion
of grants, especially for technical assistance. Interdependence was fortified by a highly protectionist
trading system. Trade between France and her former
colonies was encouraged by extensive trade preferences,
stabilization funds for agricultural exports of the
African territories, and guaranteed minimum prices
in the French market for certain commodities. With
the establishment of the EEC, France had to eliminate
most price supports and volume guarantee in favor
of tariff preferences granted by the European Six.
Although these trade advantages are to some extent
offset by the obligation of African countries to
import manufactured goods at higher than world prices,
there has been a net transfer to resources to Africa
that does not appear in France's aid figures.

Another objective of the franc zone, besides
the free flow of goods, was the free movement of
capital. This was helped by having local francs
completely convertible into French francs and local
currencies guaranteed by the French Treasury. This
guarantee was, at least in theory, an open-ended

TABLE 2

French Official Bilateral Aid Flows to Traditionally
French Areas, 1962-67
(net of amortization; million $)

Area	1962	1963	1964	1965	1966	1967
Franc Zone, Africa[1]	728.9	648.4	607.9	516.6	471.0	497.2
Cambodia, Laos, Vietnam	8.1	8.0	9.1	16.0	16.3	19.2
French Overseas Territories and Departments, Latin America	64.5	87.2	118.6	94.4	138.5	145.7
French Overseas Territories, Oceania[2]	18.9	18.1	24.2	31.0	30.6	26.7
Total Traditionally French Areas	820.4	761.7	759.8	658.0	656.4	688.8
Other Countries[3]	40.4	59.7	50.6	66.5	59.8	98.4
Total Official Bilateral Aid	860.8	821.4	810.4	724.5	716.2	787.2
Aid to Traditionally French Areas as Percentage of Total	95.3	92.8	93.7	90.8	91.6	87.5

1. French franc area, south of the Sahara (African and Malagasy States, French overseas territories and departments), Algeria, Morocco, Tunisia.

2. Data on aid to French overseas territoties in Oceania are not available separately for the period 1962-64 and are included in "unallocated" flows to Oceania. However, the other components of this "unallocated" flow are unlikely to be significant.

3. Includes unallocated flows.

Source: OECD, Geographical Distribution of Financial Flows to Less Developed Countries 1960-64, 1965, and 1966-67.

commitment: franc zone countries had an unlimited
claim on French resources and only a slightly smaller
claim on French foreign exchange reserves because
there were no special restrictions on the use of
French francs bought with local currencies in the
Paris foreign exchange market. But in fact the
French had, and still have, in the African and Malagasy
States (the States, for short), considerable control
over the monetary policies of the Franc zone countries.

French influence over development and development thinking remains greatest in the States, that
is, the region south of the Sahara that was formerly
part of French Africa. Having created states highly
dependent on French men and capital, France has been
trying to reverse her position by creating self-
reliant economies and societies. Even though the
States are independent, it is relatively easy for
France do do so because French aid is the biggest
source of investment there. French administrators,
often paid direct from France, are still very numerous and powerful in their administrations; and France
provides budgetary support for many of the states.

The emphasis is on greater self-sufficiency
in the States. The French want greater Africanization.
After independence a number of French personnel were
withdrawn in agreement with the States, but in many
countries the Africans later asked that Frenchmen
return. Also, the French are helping to develop
educational and administrative systems which are
more appropriate to local conditions. In education,
for example, research in France and in Africa has
shown that the same teaching methods have different
effects in France and in Africa; in particular, the
French have been trying to reduce the academic content
in African education and to encourage more practical
and vocational teaching. But in spite of these
attempts, the educational system in the States has
so far deviated only in minor respects from that of
France. French examinations and French curricula
still tend to impose educational uniformity on formerly
French Africa. The French have also done many economic
and other studies which they are using as the basis.

of development plans for the States. Aid is given
on the basis of these plans. France is also trying
to avoid giving assistance for nonproductive projects
which impose heavy recurrent expenses beyond the
capacity of the States to pay.

In assessing projects, France has tended to
favor those which are efficient by commercial criteria.
There does not appear to be a positive policy of using
local materials and local labor, although the French
are encouraging countries to take the problem of
unemployment more seriously. These projects are
frequently executed by public or semipublic specialized organizations.

GERMAN AID

The influence of German financial aid on the
development policies of those countries receiving
it has been small. There are several reasons for
this. One is, quite simply, that Germany has been
a full-fledged member of the aid-giving community
for only a decade. France and Britian, on the other
hand, have been giving development aid since before
the war--Britian since 1929. Another is that Germany
has no traditional sphere of influence on which it
would be natural for her to concentrate. As a result,
no single aid recipient is wholly or largely dependent on German aid, as can be seen from Table 3.
About 22 percent of German aid went to Africa in
1967, having risen considerably from the insignificant
proportion of slightly more than 1 percent in 1960.

One consequence is that German is not widely
spoken in less developed countries; this the essential
element in the transfer of ideas, a common language,
is missing. Another consequence is that Germany has
been extremely reluctant to get deeply involved with
the wider aspects of development in recipient countries; indeed, noninterference in the domestic affairs
of recipient countries has become an article of faith
in German aid policy. Germany therefore has tended
to adopt a banking approach to aid, giving almost
exclusively project aid, looking at each project in

isolation and giving the aid, provided the project
satisfies certain economic, commercial, and managerial
criteria.

But German aid carries a definite message. Just
as early American aid was dominated by Marshall Plan
thinking, so the Germans entered the aid field elated
by the success of their own economic recovery and
convinced that free enterprise and development governed
by the principles of a soziale Marktwirtschaft would
produce similar results in less developed countries.
The message is embodied in the profusion of criteria
which a project must satisfy before it qualifies for
German aid. One important principle is that the
recipient country must share in the responsibility,
political and administrative as well as financial,
for German aid projects. For this reason the Germans
usually insist that there be a local contribution to
the project. Also, the Germans particularly favor
projects which enable them to withdraw after a short
period. This is another reason for the preference
for a local stake in projects. It also explains
the German emphasis on counterpart training to replace
German technical assistance personnel. The Germans
have in addition been very keen on financial discipline;
and this is the justification of the high proportion
of loans, the terms of which have become softer.
Another principle of German aid, although not strictly
applied in practice, is that aid should not be given
to help governments in less developed countries to
do things that in Germany are done by private enterprise. Besides these principles related to projects,
the federal government has stated that countries
which run well-ordered general economic policies,
e.g., by controlling inflation, by encouraging capital
formation, by reforming their tax systems, and so
on, would receive preference in the allocation of
German aid.

But in spite of all the very careful thinking
that has gone into the German aid program, it is
doubtful whether the message has gotten across.
Perhaps conditions in underdeveloped countries made
them unreceptive to the free enterprise creed, although the public sector in countries which declare

themselves "socialist" is in fact often relatively
small. Anyhow, the methods chosen to put the message
across were not really capable of doing it. It is
very difficult for a donor country to influence
general development policy in the recipient country
through project selection because of the fungibility
of development funds. In the same way, no doubt, the
recipients of German aid have been able to get German
aid without changing their policies simply by sub-
mitting for German help those projects which satisfy
the German criteria. Projects which do not, can be
financed by other donors or out of the country's
own funds. The fact that few donors are heavily
dependent on German aid makes this all the easier.

German technical assistance has probably been
more influential than her capital aid. Many African
students are attracted to study in Germany because
of the ease of entry into German universities, once
formal qualifications have been met, and because of
the high reputation of German engineering and applied
sciences teaching. In 1967, 23,632 students and
trainees were receiving education in Germany, many
of them supporting themselves. The emphasis has,
however, shifted toward more local training. German
technical assistance, like American, has been based
on the principle of "help toward self-help." About
a third of the funds have been spent on pilot projects
which are intended as models which the recipient
can copy and multiply for himself. But even the
technical training institutes, which are another
important element in the German technical assistance
program, are regarded as pilot projects as well as
educational institutions. The objective of most
of these institutes is to turn out middle-grade
skilled men who can apply themselves to a fairly
wide range of tasks. The results have not always
worked out like this. In some cases institutes have
been established with little concern for local
conditions. In other cases the critics claim that
the projects have been overambitious. But by and
large, German technical assistance has moved in the
right direction.

German aid to Africa has increased steadily and
remained a fairly constant proportion at 10-15 percent

TABLE 3

Geographical Distribution and Chief
Recipients of German Assistance, 1960-67
(official bilateral flows, net of
amortization; million $)

	1960	1961	1962
Africa South of Sahara	5.3	13.3	59.2
Africa North of Sahara	-2.5	-4.6	4.9
Total Africa	2.8	8.7	64.1
UAR	-2.7	-4.7	3.2
Ghana	0.05	0.03	2.20
Kenya	0.01	0.03	0.01
Liberia	0.84	9.52	44.42
Somalia	0.01	0.05	2.05
Tanzania	Negligible	0.01	0.14
Nigeria	0.09	0.01	0.09
Asia	147.8	207.2	158.4
Iran	0.35	0.03	8.60
Israel	62.6	65.5	59.9
Afghanistan	0.65	3.38	2.15
Ceylon	0.55	0.47	0.71
India	82.8	131.8	54.1
Pakistan	0.16	5.3	19.7
Indonesia	-0.11	-0.25	3.58
South Korea	Negligible	0.01	0.28
Thailand	0.07	0.09	0.45
Latin America	23.2	30.6	37.6
Argentina	12.3	14.9	-1.6
Brazil	1.26	15.27	4.19
Chile	7.3	1.0	29.4
Peru	0.04	0.09	0.11
Europe	53.9	56.9	27.9
Turkey	31.3	22.3	23.1
Total	241.6	329.1	347.4
Africa's Share as Percentage of Total	1.2	2.6	18.5

1963	1964	1965	1966	1967
54.1	41.4	61.2	95.7	74.2
12.3	24.5	31.6	18.2	31.3
66.4	65.9	93.4	115.6	106.0
10.9	21.6	9.5	10.2	10.2
1.02	2.98	3.38	9.08	15.30
3.43	4.44	1.5	2.0	4.2
21.98	2.82	8.6	23.0	0.7
4.03	7.51	4.1	2.5	2.9
2.79	9.14	4.2	6.2	63.6
0.82	0.64	4.3	10.6	9.5
193.3	239.9	226.3	223.5	241.5
5.76	6.79	5.10	8.2	9.9
68.2	61.8	74.9	58.9	40.4
2.81	6.63	15.8	16.4	9.4
2.56	1.32	2.4	6.0	9.9
44.5	72.3	44.5	55.4	55.2
42.0	46.0	42.3	35.6	27.5
7.56	14.17	15.1	4.8	45.4
3.45	10.68	4.5	6.0	12.8
1.16	7.5	8.2	17.6	9.6
36.4	6.1	45.4	46.0	57.2
1.6	−15.2	−20.2	−2.2	16.5
18.70	11.66	47.35	−4.4	−4.2
7.6	4.6	−8.3	26.8	21.2
0.26	0.32	18.7	15.5	13.5
40.4	24.1	38.7	37.0	42.6
28.8	16.5	23.3	17.1	16.3
398.9	413.3	432.2	449.6	480.4
16.6	15.9	21.6	25.7	22.1

    Source: OECD, Geographical Distribution of Financial Flows to Less
Developed Countries, 1960-64, 1965, 1966-67.

of total capital aid and 43.5 percent of technical
assistance over 1956-67, 38.9 percent in 1967. The
main obstacle is said to have been the difficulty
of identifying suitable projects, although there is
also some fear of providing more technical assistance
to help in the preparation of projects, less this
lead to increased pressure for more capital aid.
There is the possibility of a vicious circle: capital
aid not rising as fast as it otherwise would because
of lack of projects, and aid for the preparation of
projects being withheld because of fears of pressure
to provide the money for the project. A multilateriza-
tion of project preparation by consultants drawn
from an international list of genuinely independent
consulting firms of high repute would help.

     In the medium-term public expenditure projections,
the Germans propose an annual increase of 7.2 percent
in official aid, while total public expenditure is
expected to grow only by 5.5 percent. German Chan-
cellor Brandt pledged the federal government to
"endeavor to attain the aim envisaged in the [Pearson]
report for a public share in development aid by an
annual average increase rate of 11 percent." In
its memorandum for the Development Assistance Committee of the OECD annual audit, the federal government says:

     Expenditure of development aid, insofar as
     it is included in the allocation of the
     Federal Ministry for Economic Cooperation,
     is to be increased from approximately,
     1,656 million Marks in 1967 to roughly
     2,555 million Marks by 1971. This repre-
     sents an average annual increase of 11.4
     percent. This increase is almost twice
     as high as the growth of the government's
     total expenditure, which is to go up at
     the rate of just 6 percent annually. . . .[2]

Since bilateral capital aid is assumed to remain
fairly constant, the growth is attributable largely
to technical assistance and multilateral aid, including contributions to the European Development
Fund (EDF). This reflects the policy decision that
highest priority should be given to technical assistance and multilateral aid.

BRITISH AID

British aid to Africa amounted to over £70 million, or about 37 percent of the total bilateral aid program of £189 million, in 1967. Most British official economic aid to Africa is provided in the form of direct bilateral assistance to individual countries, but a substantial proportion flows through contributions to the International Bank for Recon- struction and Development (IBRD), the International Development Association (IDA), and United Nations funds--the multilateral aid channels.

For historical reasons, the bulk of British aid is directed to Commonwealth countries. For example, at the end of 1967, over 11,000 publicly financed British personnel were serving the govern- ments of Commonwealth countries in Africa. In addi- tion, a direct British responsibility continues for the remaining British dependencies in the African region (Seychelles and St. Helena). Postindependence aid agreements were negotiated with Mauritius (March, 1968) and Swaziland (December, 1968).

British bilateral economic aid is extended to African countries in the form of grants, loans, and technical assistance. Much of this aid is channeled through the Special Commonwealth African Assistance Plan, formed in 1960 in order to focus attention on the aid being given by the Commonwealth to Commonwealth countries in Africa and to encourage its expansion. Table 4 shows the distribution by types as aid.

Of British bilateral aid to African countries in 1967, 17 percent was wholly tied to British goods and services, compared with 35 percent of such aid to all developing countries. If partly tied aid is included, these percentages rise 43 percent and 52 percent, respectively.

Technical assistance, valued at £18.2 million in 1967, accounts for about a quarter of total British bilateral aid to Africa. Although most of this aid went to Commonwealth countries, a significant increase

TABLE 4

British Bilateral Economic Aid to Africa, 1967
(million £)

Aid	Amount	
	1967	1970
Grants		
Technical Assistance	18	20.3
Grants to Dependencies Under Colonial Development and Welfare Acts	2	
Other Grant Aid (including budgetary support)	27	11.5
	47	31.8
Loans		
Aid for Pensions and Compensation for Former Expatriate Officials	3	0.7
Loans to Dependencies Under Colonial Development and Welfare Acts	1	23.6
Investment by Commonwealth Development Corporation	5	4.5
Loans Under Export Guarantees Act (1949)	5	0.7
	23	29.5
Total	70	61.3

Source: Aid for Development, Fact Sheet Overseas Development Ministry for 1967 and Overseas Development Administration of U.K. Foreign and Commonwealth Office.

Note: A major development in British aid policy was the decision in June, 1965 that development loans would be made interest-free to countries whose economic circumstances justified this concession. Since then (and up to the end of 1970) the following large interest-free loans have been made to African countries: Ethiopia (£2 million), Kenya (£3 million in 1965, £18 million for 1966-70 and £11.5 million from 1970), Malawi (£7 million for 1966-68 and £5 million for 1969-70), Uganda (£5.5 million from 1966, £1 million in 1968 and £5.5 million in 1969), Sierra Leone (£1.8 million in 1970), Botswana (£4.4 million in 1970), Swaziland (£4.5 million in 1970), The Gambia (£3.2 million for 1967-71), Nigeria (£10.5 million in 1968 and £1 million in 1969), Mauritius (£1 million in 1969 and £5 million for 1970-71) and Ghana (£5.4 million for 1969-70 and £3.7 million for 1970-71).

is now taking place in disbursements to non-Commonwealth countries.

Technical assistance includes the provision
of British staff and experts; training for Africans
in Britain; services of the Directorate of Overseas
Surveys and the Overseas Division of the Institute
of Geological Sciences; equipment for instructional
purposes or for British experts; small capital grants
for buildings in which British experts are working;
and British consultancies and assistance in the
fields of education and research.

By far the most important item of technical
assistance in Africa (12 Million in 1967) is the
aid given under Overseas Service Aid Scheme (OSAS)
and similar schemes, which, by contributing to the
cost of British personnel employed by overseas governments, enables them to retain and recruit expert
staff from Britain until local staff can be trained
to take over. There were nearly 10,800 British officers in posts in Africa at the end of 1967 under
these arrangements.

In addition 500 British-paid technical assistance
experts and teachers (wholly in British service)
were serving in posts in Africa at the end of 1967.
There were also 944 volunteers subsidized from British
government funds under the 1967/68 program. At the
same time, there were 1,815 Africans in training
in Britain paid for from British public funds: 1,333
under tenchical assistance regional program, 387
under Commonwealth Education Cooperation, and 95
under British Council programs. In addition (over
18,500) Africans students not financed from public
funds were enrolled in courses in Britain in 1966/67.

In some African countries, where increases in
budgetary expenditure, in the short run at least,
exceed practicable increases in revenue, Britain,
has met the need for budgetary assistance. Malawi,
for example, has received aid of this kind since
becoming independent in 1964: for the three years
1968-70 Britain undertook to provide a maximum of
£3.3, £2.8, and £2.2 million a year, respectively.
Other countries in the African region which have

TABLE 5

British And DAC Aid to Less
Developed Countries, 1962-67

	1962			1963			1964		
	From U.K.	Total Rec'd DAC Countries	Percent	From U.K.	Total Rec'd DAC Countries	Percent	From U.K.	Total Rec'd DAC Countries	Percent
Africa									
Basutoland (Lesotho	5.7	5.7	100.0	5.4	5.5	98.1	5.4	5.5	98.1
Bechuanaland (Botswana)	5.2	5.2	100.0	5.3	5.3	100.0	8.8	8.8	100.0
Gambia	2.5	2.5	100.0	5.1	5.1	100.0	2.4	2.5	96.0
Ghana	.1	5.5	1.8	3.2	17.2	18.6	6.6	19.1	34.6
Kenya	43.1	48.5	88.9	47.8	54.7	87.4	48.0	55.2	87.0
Malawi	11.6	11.6	100.0	16.4	16.5	99.4	30.2	32.3	93.4
Mauritius	4.1	4.1	100.0	5.5	5.5	100.0	1.9	2.0	95.0
Nigeria	16.9	30.0	99.4	2.0	18.8	10.6	11.6	42.7	27.2
Rhodesia	-	-		10.8	10.9	99.1	4.2	4.4	95.5
Seychelles	.5	.5	100.0	.6	.6	100.0	.9	.9	100.0
Sierra Leone	5.7	7.8	173.1	6.4	9.5	67.4	5.2	8.7	59.8
Swaziland	5.0	5.0	100.0	5.5	5.5	100.0	12.4	12.4	100.0
Tanzania	37.7	47.0	80.2	23.2	30.5	76.1	24.7	41.8	59.1
Uganda	25.0	28.1	90.0	17.6	19.8	88.9	16.8	19.4	86.6
Zambia	5.9	5.9	100.0	5.4	5.4	100.0	20.6	20.7	99.5

	1965			1966			1967	
From U.K.	Total Rec'd DAC Countries	Percent	From U.K.	Total Rec'd DAC Countries	Percent	From U.K.	Total Rec'd DAC Countries	Percent
8.86	9.25	95.8	10.8	11.0	98.2	11.0	12.4	90.0
9.41	9.45	99.6	12.9	16.0	80.6	15.2	16.6	91.6
3.90	4.16	93.7	2.3	92.0	2.4	2.4	2.8	85.7
1.25	44.63	2.8	1.0	76.5	1.3	0.9	67.2	1.3
53.26	69.35	76.8	31.1	55.3	56.2	20.6	32.1	64.2
30.43	34.53	88.1	24.7	30.7	80.5	23.0	29.0	80.0
1.67	1.86	90.0	3.8	3.9	97.4	4.5	4.7	95.7
26.55	67.84	39.1	16.0	72.0	22.2	13.3	70.5	18.9
3.23	3.56	90.7	0.1	0.3	33.3	0.2	0.3	66.6
			0.9	0.9	100.0	2.2	2.2	100.0
2.68	17.08	15.7	3.3	11.9	27.9	2.1	6.6	31.8
14.99	15.05	99.6	10.1	10.2	100.0	8.9	9.2	96.7
17.77	34.93	50.9	11.7	37.3	30.3	2.7	30.6	8.8
13.32	19.17		12.1	24.0	50.4	13.2	20.4	64.7
12.07	13.16	91.7	26.7	33.7	79.2	40.1	68.3	60.0

Continued

TABLE 5 (Continued)

	1962			1963			1964		
	From U.K	Total Rec'd DAC Countries	Percent	From U.K	Total Rec'd DAC Countries	Percent	From U.K.	Total Rec'd DAC Countries	Percent
South Asia									
Ceylon	2.1	12.8	16.4	2.0	10.7	18.7	1.4	9.4	14.9
India	62.0	666.7	9.3	57.7	902.9	6.4	94.6	1113.5	8.5
Nepal	.3	8.3	3.6	1.4	15.7	8.9	1.2	18.5	6.5
Pakistan	17.8	377.7	4.7	26.3	483.4	5.4	28.0	493.9	5.7
Far East									
Malaysia	9.2	21.5	42.8	3.7	11.3	32.7	9.8	14.2	6.9
Singapore	.6	.7	85.7	.1	.4	25.0	.3	.4	75.0
Middle East									
Bahrein	1.3	1.3	100.0	.6	.6	100.0	.6	.6	100.0
Jordan	7.8	60.9	12.8	6.1	63.0	9.7	8.0	54.7	14.6
Muscat and Oman	.4	.4	100.0	.4	.4	100.0	4.0	4.0	100.0
South Arabia Federation	11.7	11.7	100.0	12.9	12.9	100.0	16.3	16.3	100.0
Trucial Oman	.4	.4	100.0	.4	.4	100.0	.3	.3	100.0

	1965			1966			1967		
From U.K.	Total Rec'd DAC Countries	Percent	From U.K.	Total Rec'd DAC Countries	Percent	From U.K.	Total Rec'd DAC Countries	Percent	
0.25	13.62	-1.8	6.6	30.9	21.4	11.0	45.4	24.4	
65.36	1083.13	60.3	89.4	1082.3	8.2	74.3	1142.9	6.5	
0.10	16.96	0.6	1.1	12.3	8.9	1.1	13.1	8.4	
28.26	453.72	6.2	24.0	341.7	7.0	27.2	426.0	6.4	
11.08	20.62	53.8	13.1	27.2	48.2	9.0	21.4	42.1	
0.91	2.15	42.3	0.4	1.6	25.0	4.6	6.7	68.7	
0.88	0.88	100.0	0.9	0.9	100.0	0.1	0.1	100.0	
8.20	46.87	17.5	7.3	52.5	13.9	5.9	30.4	19.4	
0.10	0.10	100.0	0.6	0.6	100.0	0.9	0.9	100.0	
26.03	26.03	99.9	29.7	29.7	100.0	22.8	22.8	100.0	
1.49	1.49	100.0	1.3	1.3	100.0	1.5	1.5	100.0	

Source: OECD, Geographical Distribution of Financial Flows to Less Developed Countries, 1960-64, 1966-67.

received budgetary aid from Britain include Gambia,
Lesotho, Botswana, Swaziland, St. Helena, and the
Seychelles.

In many African countries, where development
programs are concentrated largely in the agricultural
and educational sectors, a comparatively high proportion of development expenditure has to go to
defray local costs and hence, indirectly, imports,
rather than to pay directly for imports. Britain
provides some untied aid which can be used for this
purpose or, when the aid is tied, it may be tied to
goods and services either from Britain or from the
recipient country. But the proportion of aid devoted
to this purpose is too small to avoid serious distortions in the direction of excessive capital intensity and excessive direct import content.

A special type of British aid to Africa has
been the financing of major schemes of land transfer
and settlement in Kenya, where a large European farming
community previously enjoyed exclusive rights to own
land in scheduled areas. For several schemes (including the Million Acre Scheme) for the transfer of
mixed farming land from European to African ownership,
beginning in 1961/62, the British government agreed
to provide over £22 million. (See Chapter 4 for
reasons why this is not counted as aid.) In addition,
loans of £3 million were made available during 1963-
66 for the Kenya Land Bank and Agricultural Finance
Corporation to assist land transactions outside the
settlement areas. Further disbursements, in the
form of an £18 million interest-free loan for the
period 1966-70, followed the report of a mission
led by Maxwell Stamp. It was estimated that just
over one-third of this sum will be spent on financing the annual transfer of 100,000 acres of mixed
farming land; the balance will be devoted to general
development, including land consolidation.

Assistance for higher education in Africa has
always been a prominent feature of British aid.
Many of the universities and technical colleges
have been founded and developed with British capital.
For example, by 1967 Britain had provided about

£3.7 million to Makerere University College; £1.7 million to University College, Nairobi; £1 million to the University of Zambia; £1 million to the University of Malawi; £1.5 million to the University of Botswana, Lesotho, and Swaziland; and about £300,000 to help establish the new University of Mauritius. In addition, Britain made a £5 million capital grant for postsecondary education developments in Nigeria. In non-Commonwealth Africa, assistance with the provision of staff and equipment has been given to the universities at Khartoum, Addis Ababa, Monrovia, Yaounde, and Abidjan. Assistance with regard to recruitment and general academic advice are provided by the Inter-University Council for Higher Education Overseas and the Council for Technical Education and Training for Overseas Countries, whose budgets are provided by the Ministry of Overseas Development.

Through its contribution to United Nations funds, Britain supports the work of the ECA, which endeavors to promote a regional and subregional approach to African problems and to render increasing services to African governments. Some British technical assistance has also been given directly to regional projects sponsored or undertaken by the ECA. British aid also goes to the East African Community (Kenya, Uganda, Tanzania), and technical assistance is being given to the Association of West African states. Capital aid and technical assistance have been given or pledged for the international anti-rinderpest campaign sponsored by the Scientific, Technical and Research Commission of the Organization of African Unity (OAU), which has also received British technical assistance in other activities. British technical assistance to the Desert Locust Control Organization for Eastern Africa has recently been increased. In addition, Britain had indicated its willingness to give help to the African Development Bank.

One criticism that can be raised against British aid to Africa, is that tying to British procurement and the inadequate provision for local costs (i.e., in-direct foreign exchange costs to which projects give rise when local resources are employed) have encouraged excessively capital-intensive and import-intensive

TABLE 6

British Government Bilateral Disbursements of
Economic Aid to Africa, 1957-58 to 1965-66
(million $)

	1957-58			1964-65				1965-66			
	Grants	Loans	Total	Grants	Loans	Technical Assistance	Total	Grants	Loans	T.A.	Total
Africa	52.3	10.0	62.3	95.7	83.9	50.2	229.8	76.9	97.2	55.6	229.7
Commonwealth	39.5	10.0	49.5	84.6	79.1	49.4	213.1	76.6	91.5	54.2	223.3
Others	12.8	--	12.8	11.1	4.8	0.8	16.7	0.3	5.7	1.4	7.4

Source: Ministry of Overseas Development, Overseas Development; The Work in Hand (August, 1965; January, 1967).

TABLE 7

British Bilateral Aid Program
Disbursements to Africa,
1967 and 1968
(gross and net of amortization; million £)

	1967		1968	
	Gross	Net	Gross	Net
Commonwealth Africa	57.67	54.08	63.17	59.09
Non-Commonwealth Africa	1.237	1.227	1.237	0.804

Bilateral Technical Assistance Disbursements

	1967	1968
Commonwealth Africa	17.6	20.8
Non-Commonwealth Africa	0.56	0.87

Source: Ministry of Overseas Development,
British Aid Statistics (1964-68).

projects and have thereby contributed to the growth
of unemployment, to unequal income distribution, and
to waste of indigenous resources. The sectoral distribution has tended to favor infrastructure and
industry; and even the relatively small share allocated
to agriculture has been too capital-intensive (e.g.,
tractors to Uganda), although the agricultural schemes
of the Commonwealth Development Corporation in Kenya,
Uganda, Tanzania, Swaziland, Nigeria, Cameroon, and
elsewhere have pioneered the way in projects which
have benefited the small farmer. British aid has
also failed to force the pace of regional and subregional integration. A reluctance to appear neocolonial has led to possibly excessive susceptibility
to economic nationalism.

British aid, and especially educational aid,
might be also criticized for having reacted too

violently to any possible charge of neocolonialism.
The elites in power in former British colonies have
been deeply imbued with outdated British values and
attitudes, and great respect for their preferences
leads to a reflection of the values and attitudes
of the British ruling class some decades ago. A
legacy of British colonialism is the imprint of an
educational system and its values and ideals, which
are those of a small ruling class in a by gone world.
The emphasis on liberal arts, the status of manual
and agricultural work, the emphasis on elitism, the
high regard for administration, and the low status
of business management are all parts of an ethos
which is not favorable to development in the last
quarter of the twentieth century. African salary
structures, African educational systems, African
employment preferences, and African aid requests
reflect this ethos to some extent, and it could be
argued that greater interference and paternalism
might be justified as an antidote to these outdated
systems and standards. (For criticism of the treatment of pensions to former colonial civil servants,
see Chapter 4.)

The value of this educational aid has recently
undergone a thorough criticism. The design of the
universities and their function in the development
process and the life of the community; the allocation
of funds between recurrent and capital expenditure;
the neglect of middle-level vocational training and
education, of adult education, and of rural education;
and the low quality of an excessively rapidly expanding primary system of education have rightly been
criticized. The British Ministry of Overseas Development has recently subjected its educational aid to
Africa to a thorough and fundamental review. If
the new administration follows along the lines of
this review--and it appears that these policies are
bipartisan--there is good reason to believe that some
of the faults will be corrected. A DAC expert group
on aid to education in Africa has also identified
the faults of past policy and made recommendations
for changes.[3]

UNITED STATES AID

A belief in the harmony between self-interest
and altruism dominates much of Anglo-Saxon thinking.
It is in moral philosophy the equivalent of empircism
in epistemology. One is reminded of Bishop Butler's
famous words: "When we sit down in a cool hour, we
can neither justify to ourselves this or any other
pursuit, till we are convinced that it will be to
our own happiness. . . ." It is puzzling that it
appears easier to identify, or at least harmonize,
individual happiness with the national interest
than with that of the world community. A moral,
disinterested concern by rich countries with the
development of the poor is hardly ever conceded and,
if it were, would probably be dismissed as hypocrisy.
But as hypocrisy is the tribute vice pays to virtue,
so professions of national self-interest (political,
strategic, or commercial) in the development of
poor countries may be the tribute that virtue has
to pay to vice, possibly the virtue of the administration to the vice of the legislators, the electorate,
and what is thought to be public opinion.

The United States declares that aid is an in-
strument of U.S. foreign policy. The purpose of
aid is to promote development. But development, for
it, is not an end in itself: it is a means to the
establishment and maintenance of free, democratic,
peaceful, societies. Political security and economic
stability are seen as the results of development
aid. It is not our task here to examine the truth
of this proposition.

Emphasis has shifted, in the course of time,
from short-term political gain to economic and social
development. The choice of the countries which should
receive aid is influenced by stronger political
considerations than the use of the aid once it has
been allocated to a particular country.

Another fundamental tenet of the American aid
philosophy is that aid is given to end aid. Rostowian
terminology of "takeoff into self-sustained growth"

provides the intellectual underpinning of this
philosophy. It seems, on the face of it, to conflict
with the alleged desire to reduce income gaps, for
this would indicate an allocation of aid by different
criteria and would suggest continuation of aid programs
until the gaps had disappeared.

Two additional features distinguish the American
aid program from those of other donors: strong
representation in the recipient country and emphasis
on recipients' self-help. Both lead to a careful
consideration of "performance criteria" of developing
countries and a tendency to impose what are conceived
to be the correct policies in order to ensure the
effective use of aid. Where Britain, for instance,
proclaims the need for recipient countries to choose
and identify priorities, America has few hesitations
in laying down appropriate priorities for them.

At first, self-help and performance criteria
were derived from general principles and applied
fairly universally. They included the preparation
of development plans, reform of land tenure and tax
structure, fiscal and institutional measures to raise
domestic savings, monetary policies that avoided
quantitative restrictions, scope for private investment, and so on. But with growing experience, the
diverse conditions in particular countries were more
fully taken into account and specific recommendations
made, often in accordance with the recommendations
of the International Monetary Fund (IMF) and the
IBRD.

MEDIUM-SCALE DONORS

Although Canada, the Netherlands, Belgium, and
the Scandinavian countries have established channels
of aid to one African country or to a group of countries, these donors, being small, prefer multilateral
channels. Since they are now more likely to raise
their aid efforts than the big donors, African countries would have to increase their share from the United
Nations Development Program (UNDP), IBRD, IDA, etc.,

to benefit from the growing aid efforts to these
countries.

AID PROGRAMS OF CENTRALLY PLANNED ECONOMIES

Reported commitments of credits to the developing countries from the centrally planned economies
in 1967 were the lowest for four years and had dropped
to 45 percent of the peak figure of 1966. The main
reduction was in credits pledged by the USSR, which
had been at a record level of over $1 billion in
1966. (Some of these were advance commitments.)

Commitments of Africa moved inversely to total
commitments and reached their lowest level, $46
million in 1966, a considerable drop from the 1964
peak of $874 million. However, this trend was re-
versed in 1967; and, at $428 million, commitments
in that year were the highest since 1964. They included two sizable credits to Algeria: $120 million
from East Germany for the purchase of agricultural
and industrial equipment and $50 million from
Czechoslovakia. The latter also offered credits
of $19 million each to Morocco and the Sudan, while
East Germany, Poland, and Rumania granted credits
to the UAR equivalent to $86 million, $20 million,
and $14 million, respectively. One of the largest
single credits of 1967, the equivalent of $100 million,
was pledged to Nigeria by Czechoslovakia, Poland, the
USSR, and Yugoslavia.

The chief African recipients of aid from the
centrally planned economies have been Algeria and
the UAR. Over the period 1963-68, these two countries accounted for about 71 percent of commitments
to Africa.

As can be seen from Table 10, commitments of
the centrally planned economies to Africa show great
year-to-year fluctuation except for the UAR.

TABLE 8

U.S. Loans and Grants to Africa, 1962-70
(million $; U.S. fiscal years)

Program	1962	1963	1964	1965	1966	1967	1968	1969	1970
Official Development Assistance									
AID: Total	315.4	240.3	189.0	150.5	171.5	186.3	115.1	107.7	138.6
Loans	116.0	117.1	90.9	73.7	90.9	107.1	55.1	29.0	54.7
Grants	199.4	123.2	98.1	76.8	80.6	79.2	60.5	78.7	83.9
Food for Peace: Total	96.9	199.8	127.7	108.2	128.4	147.1	137.2	172.7	108.3
Title I: Total Sales									
Agreement	40.8	58.9	44.3	52.9	36.0	54.5	43.5	17.5	3.8
Planned for U.S. Use	10.0	9.7	13.2	16.3	7.8	14.1	7.9	2.9	0.6
Planned for Country Use	30.8	49.2	31.1	36.6	28.2	40.4	35.6	14.6	3.2
Loans for Economic Development	19.0	20.3	27.0	30.6	27.4	37.8	31.1	12.9	1.2
Grants for Economic Development	11.6	27.9	0.9	0.9	--	--	--	--	--
Grants for Common Defense	-	-	-	3.9	--	--	--	--	--
Cooley Loans	0.2	1.0	3.1	1.2	0.9	2.6	4.3	1.7	0.2
Title II: Emergency Relief, Economic Development, World Food	47.2	112.2	42.2	31.6	41.3	40.9	31.8	94.6	46.2
Voluntary Relief	18.2	37.4	52.4	31.5	26.2	32.1	22.6	23.1	26.1
Other Official Development Assistance (mainly Peace Corps)	7.3	14.9	24.9	27.2	32.7	25.7	23.7	22.0	20.2
Total Official Development Assistance	419.6	455.0	341.6	285.9	332.7	359.1	276.4	302.4	267.1
Loans	135.9	139.4	121.0	114.0	151.9	181.2	137.7	84.0	88.9
Grants	283.7	315.6	220.5	171.9	180.8	177.9	138.8	218.4	178.1
Other Official									
Export-Import Bank Long-Term Loans	45.3	6.9	12.2	34.3	30.9	5.0	41.9	54.7	27.4
Total Economic Assistance	464.9	461.9	353.8	320.2	363.6	364.1	318.3	357.1	294.5
Loans	181.2	146.3	133.2	148.3	182.8	186.2	179.6	138.7	116.3
Grants	283.7	315.6	220.5	171.9	180.8	177.9	138.8	218.4	178.1

Source: AID, Statistics and Reports Division, US Overseas Loans and Grants and Assistance from International Organizations: Obligations and Loan Authorizations. July 1, 1945 June 30, 1970. Special report prepared for the House Foreign Affairs Committee.

TABLE 9

Geographical Distribution and Chief African Recipients of U.S. Assistance, 1960-67
(official bilateral flows, net of amortization, $ million)

	1960	1961	1962	1963	1964	1965	1966	1967
Africa North of Sahara	258.0	316.0	337.0	316.0	319.0	201.1	161.0	87.0
Africa South of Sahara	39.0	75.0	197.0	159.0	161.0	248.0	276.0	221.0
Total Africa[1]	297.0	392.0	536.0	480.0	489.0	461.2	455.0	329.0
Algeria	1.0	2.0	38.0	39.0	43.0	7.4	23.0	11.0
Libya	33.0	24.0	20.0	16.0	6.0	2.6	1.0	-2.0
Morocco	60.0	98.0	49.0	49.0	39.0	51.4	47.0	31.0
Tunisia	51.0	77.0	53.0	38.0	45.0	54.1	39.0	46.0
UAR[2]	113.0	115.0	177.0	174.0	186.0	85.7	51.0	1.0
Congo (Kinshasa)	Negligible	3.0	64.0	36.0	38.0	44.8	33.0	30.0
Ethiopia	8.0	14.0	23.0	19.0	9.0	11.3	21.0	12.0
French Franc Area, South of Sahara	Negligible	7.0	24.0	34.0	38.0	22.8	30.0	20.0
Ghana	2.0	2.0	2.0	13.0	8.0	33.2	62.0	33.0
Liberia	9.0	18.0	34.0	11.0	12.0	25.2	23.0	36.0
Nigeria	3.0	5.0	12.0	15.0	25.0	26.5	30.0	35.0
Sudan	16.0	17.0	11.0	9.0	9.0	9.0	2.0	5.0
Tanzania	0.3	5.0	9.0	4.0	6.0	9.2	13.0	9.0
Asia	1,722.0	1,591.0	1,755.0	2,035.0	1,993.0	2,022.9	1,968.0	2,170.0
Latin America	184.0	702.0	578.0	560.0	452.0	613.5	723.0	604.0
Europe	294.0	440.0	382.0	344.0	235.0	249.9	250.0	158.0
Total[3]	2,578.0	3,228.0	3,399.0	3,556.0	3,233.0	3,462.6	3,548.0	3,413.0
Africa's Share as Percentage of the Total	11.5	12.1	15.8	13.5	15.1	13.3	12.8	9.6

1. Including unspecified flows.
2. Includes, for 1960, grants to Syria, not available separately.
3. Including assistance to Oceania and unallocated flows.

Source: OECD, Geographical Distribution of Financial Flows To Less Developed Countries. 1960-64, 1965, 1966-67.

TABLE 10

Commitments of Bilateral Economic Assistance by
Centrally Planned Economies, 1954-68
(million $; national currencies converted into $ at
official rates of exchange)

	Total 1954-62	1963	1964	1965	1966	1967	1968*
Total Commitment	4,454	341	1,246	646	1,313	621	758
Distribution by Source							
Bulgaria	20	6	--	--	30	47	35
China (Mainland)	365	88	305	77	6	--	42
Czechoslovakia	468	20	118	43	192	88	200
East Germany	108	--	71	132	--	231	8
Hungary	151	14	10	42	52	45	40
Poland	332	8	54	22	--	63	20
Romania	112	--	70	--	--	14	45
USSR	2,898	205	618	330	1,033	133	368
Distribution by Recipient							
Africa	1,302	242	874	247	46	420	223
Algeria	--	156	143	--	--	170	--
Central African Republic	--	--	4	--	--	--	--
Congo (Brazzaville)	--	--	33	29	--	--	--
Ethiopia	114	--	--	--	--	--	--
Ghana	122	--	22	20	--	--	--
Guinea	119	--	--	--	3	--	--
Kenya	--	--	55	--	11	--	--
Mali	85	--	27	--	--	--	--
Morocco	17	--	--	--	--	19	--
Nigeria	-	--	--	14	--	84	--
Senegal	--	--	7	--	--	--	--
Somalia	74	22	--	--	6	--	--
Sudan	22	--	--	--	--	27	--
Tunisia	48	--	--	--	--	--	55
Uganda	--	--	15	15	--	--	--
UAR	701	64	517	126	--	120	168
Tanzania	--	--	51	--	26	--	--
Latin America	381	--	--	15	100	107	20
West Asia	479	75	97	33	523	64	473
Southern and Southeast Asia	2,292	24	275	351	644	30	42

*Preliminary

Source: United Nations, The External Financing of Economic Development, 1963-67, E/4652; 1964-68, E/4815.

32

MULTILATERAL AID

The complexity and scope of the development
process, as well as the pressures of particular interest groups, have given rise to several multilateral
agencies in the development field. Some specialized
international agencies originally established for
other purposes have assumed important development
functions. The proliferation of these agencies has
caused a host of new problems.

The establishment of the UN regional economic
commissions and of the regional development banks has
resulted from the awareness of the diversity of
the developing countries and regions and the consequent
need for regional and subregional differentiation
and specialization so that the best use can be made
of local knowledge. The East African Development
Bank is an illustration of an institution with a
subregional focus. Another important factor in the
growth of geographically specialized agencies has
been the desire of the developing countries for greater
influence on the international agencies.

This is one of the reasons why the ADB is
entirely financed by African contributions--the only
regional bank which only developing countries control.
However, in the words of the Pearson Report:

> The history of the past two decades has
> many examples of the efforts of the develop-
> ing countries to create institutions in
> which they would have a decisive voice, but
> all such efforts have demonstrated the dif-
> ficulty which such institutions experience
> in raising funds for their activities. A
> case in point is that of the United Nations
> Capital Development Fund which came into
> existence in 1966 after almost two decades
> of vigorous opposition and has received no
> contributions from the industrialized
> countries.[4]

The need for development finance on concessional
terms has led to the establishment of the IDA in

1960 as an affiliate of the World Bank. Unlike the
IBRD, it makes loans on very soft terms--0.75 percent
interest and 50 years' maturity. The IDA, along
with other suppliers of concessional multilateral
finance, such as the United Nations agencies, EDF,
and the concessional loan windows of the regional
development banks, depend very largely on financial
assistance from the high-income countries, whereas
such multilateral institutions as the World Bank
and the European Investment Bank (EIB), which lend on
harder terms, depend to a greater extent on the
private capital markets.

     Table 11 shows that Africa's receipts of multi-
lateral aid were $0.70 per head in 1968, of which
$0.31 is accounted for by the EDF and the European
Investment Bank EIB, most of it coming from the EDF,
which is Africa's largest source of multilateral
aid. The operations of the EDF will be discussed
later.

     It is the relatively better-off developing
countries of Europe and Latin America which show the
highest receipts per head of multilateral aid, most
of it on market terms (the IBRD accounts for more
than half the receipts in both cases). However, in
the four developing subregions with lowest average
aid per head in 1960, multilateral agencies made major
contributions to the increase in aid per head.

     The multilateral agencies greatly expanded their
contributions, increasing their share to about 10
percent of the total flow during 1964-67.

     Net multilateral flows to Africa, Asia, and Latin
America averaged $543 million over the period 1960-66.
The annual average flow to Africa was $169 million,
or 31 percent of the total.[5] The volume of multilateral assistance to Africa doubled from $125 million
in 1961 to $260 million in 1967. However, as the
total net multilateral flow more than quadrupled over
this period, Africa's share declined from about 60
percent in 1961 to about 33 percent in 1968. (See
Table 12.)

TABLE 11

Geographical Distribution of Multilateral Transfers per Head, 1968
(U.S. $)

	Europe	Africa	Latin America	Asia
Total Multilateral	1.03	.70	.96	.41
World Bank Group Total	.71	.20	.60	.32
IBRD	.53	.13	.50	.06
IFC	.02	.01	.02	.01
IDA	.16	.05	.08	.25
IDB	--	--	.17	--
African Development Bank	--	--	--	--
Asian Development Bank	--	--	--	--
EDF/EIB	.25	.31	.03	--
United Nations	.07	.20	.17	.09

Source: L. B. Pearson et al., Partners in Development, p. 213.

35

TABLE 12

Net Flow of Resources from the Multilateral Agencies to the Developing
Regions, 1961-68
(million $)

Recipient Region	1961	1962	1963	1964	1965	1966	1967	1968[a]
Africa	125	146	116	175	208	240	263	277
Latin America, Caribbean	-44	70	286	315	142	208	310	235
Southern, Southeast Asia[b]	81	123	158	171	358	290	340	280
West Asia	44	50	42	48	70	41	48	39
All Developing Countries[c]	209	398	616	720	789	802	979	844
Africa's Share as Percentage of the Total	60	37	19	24	26	30	27	33

Note: The resources are grants and loans less subscriptions, contributions, participations, and repayments. In case of technical assistance under the regular programs of United Nations agencies, contributions are imputed on the basis of scales of assessment.

[a]Preliminary; partly estimated.
[b]Including net disbursements in developing countries in the Pacific.
[c]Including interregional and unallocated flows.

Source: United Nations, The External Financing of Economic Development, 1963-67, E/4652; 1964-68, E/4815.

TABLE 13

IBRD and IDA Flows to Africa, 1960-67
(million $; net, excluding interest payments)

	1960	1961	1962	1963	1964	1965	1966	1967
IBRD	129.3	55.4	56.1	8.5	34.1	47.9	33.4	47.1
IDA	-1.5	-4.5	-6.0	-12.1	-3.6	6.0	17.7	28.2
Total	127.8	50.9	50.1	-3.6	30.5	53.9	51.1	75.3

Source: OECD, Geographical Distribution of Financial Flows, 1960-64, 1965, 1966-67.

Further increases in multilateral aid are
expected as the regional banks step up their activities and as the World Bank group doubles its lending
in the course of 1969-73. This would tend toward a
hardening of average terms, owing to the high cost
of borrowing in private capital markets, on which
the World Bank may have to depend increasingly.[6]

As can be seen from Table 13, Africa has not
gained from the considerable increase in the World
Bank group's lending operations (gross disbursement
rose from $398 million in 1960-61 to $762 million
in 1968-69). In fact, IBRD and IDA assistance to
Africa in 1967 was less than two-thirds of the 1960
level, although the 1967 level was greater than that
of any other year. If we make allowance for rising
prices and interest payments, the decline in terms
of real resource transfers will be seen to be even
greater.

Acceptance of the Pearson target for multilateral
aid (i.e., a minimum of 20 percent of total flow by
1975) would mean a vast increase, possibly fivefold,
of United Nations activities by 1975. We shall
return later to the needed reforms in the organization
of the United Nations Agencies and the regional
development banks if these institutions are to disburse
effectively such a large increase of funds.

The UNDP has done a large number of preinvestment
studies in Africa. The Jackson Report records,
depressingly, that eleven preinvestment projects,
costing the UNDP $10 million, have generated $2,300
million of later investment, one-third of it coming
from the World Bank. On present evidence, the agencies
and the banks do not have the capacity to disburse
substantially larger sums, even if they could be
raised. The main issues for the IBRD/IDA are whether
they should strengthen their local representation or
delegate increasingly to local development agencies
or contribute funds to development corporations with
local staff and local expertise; whether they should
continue to hand over projects when they are com-
pleted--precisely when the important problems of
efficient management arise; and whether they should

TABLE 14

Regional Annual Distribution of Net Official Assistance from DAC
Members and Multilateral Agencies, 1964-67 Average
(million $)

Country	Central America-Caribbean	South America	North Africa	Sub-Sahara Africa	South, West Asia	Southeast, East Asia	Total
Australia[a]	0.02	c	--	0.59	19.49	12.78	32.88
Austria	1.13	2.98	1.44	1.39	9.92	1.11	17.97
Belgium	0.07	1.16	0.83	73.83	0.63	0.09	76.61
Canada	10.64	1.07	2.00	12.27	96.86	8.86	131.70
Denmark[b]	c	0.96	0.43	2.15	2.42	0.52	6.48
France	6.28	8.35	182.85	262.20	4.75	22.75	487.18
Germany	1.82	36.45	26.40	68.10	183.34	48.71	364.82
Italy	4.68	-16.49	19.96	29.62	8.16	5.49	51.42
Japan	1.45	4.90	0.08	0.68	71.61	148.92	227.64
Netherlands	8.16	10.50	0.48	35.01	10.66	4.70	69.51
Norway	0.01	0.04	0.10	1.47	1.42	0.51	3.55
Sweden	c	0.01	1.55	6.43	7.70	6.45	22.14
Switzerland	0.10	1.21	0.41	1.53	1.40	0.18	4.83
UK	20.29	2.94	3.59	194.00	155.44	19.21	395.47
US	166.28	409.69	192.03	226.11	1,276.16	732.34	3,002.61
Total Bilateral	220.93	463.77	432.15	915.38	1.849.96	1,012.62	4,894.81
Total Multilateral Agencies	87.17	168.37	15.64	178.52	290.26	44.01	783.97
Total	308.10	632.14	447.79	1,093.90	2,140.22	1,056.63	5,678.78

Note: Definitions of the six developing regions are as follows:

Central America-Caribbean: Bahamas, Bermuda, Costa Rica, Cuba, Dominican Republic, El Salvador, Guatemala, Haiti, Honduras, British Honduras, Jamaica, Mexico, Netherlands Antilles, Nicaragua, Panama, Trinidad and Tobago, British West Indies.

South America: Argentina, Bolivia, Brazil. Chile, Colombia, Ecuador, Falkland Islands, Guyana, Paraguay, Peru, Surinam, Uruguay, Venezuela.

North Africa: Algeria, Libya, Morocco, Tunisia, United Arab Republic.

Sub-Sahara: Botswana, Burundi, Cameroon, Central African Republic, Chad, Congo (Brazzaville), Congo (Kinshasa), Dahomey, Ethiopia, Gabon, Gambia, Ghana, Guinea, Kenya, Ivory Coast, Lesotho, Liberia, Malagasy, Malawi, Mali, Mauritania, Mauritius, Niger, Nigeria, Rwanda, Senegal, Seychelles, Sierra Leone, Somalia, Sudan, Swaziland, Tanzania, Togo, Upper Volta, Uganda, Zambia.

South and West Asia: Afghanistan, Bahrein, Bhutan, Ceylon, India, Iran, Iraq, Israel, Jordan, Kuwait, Lebanon, Maldive Islands, Muscat and Oman, Nepal, Pakistan, Qatar, Saudi Arabia, South Arabia Federation, Syria, Trucial Oman, Yemen.

Southeast and East Asia: Burma, Brunei, Cambodia, China (Taiwan), Indonesia, Korea (South, Laos, Malaysia, Philippines, Singapore, Thailand, Vietnam (South).

Unallocated financial flows have been excluded from all totals.

[a]Excludes 1964 Australian donations.
[b]1965-67 average.
[c]Less than $5,000.

Source: OECD, Geographical Distribution of Financial Flows to Less Developed Countries, 1961-64, 1965, 1966-67.

move from the philosophy of project support to a more
general form of combined projects and program support.

THE EUROPEAN DEVELOPMENT FUND

The EDF dates back to the Treaty of Rome that
established EEC. Between 1958 and 1963 it made $581
million nonrepayable grants to the eighteen signatory
states in Africa and Madagascar. In the second period,
from 1964 to 1969 (under the Second Fund of the Yaoundé
Convention), the sum was raised to $730 million (with
an additional $70 million for other territories still
linked to the European members). The largest part
of this takes the form of grants. The sum of $1,000
million is envisaged for the third EDF, starting in
1970.

The investments initially were entirely in social
and economic infrastructure (roads, water, harbors,
schools, hospitals, medical services), but the second
EDF included productive projects, especially in
agriculture. The sectoral distribution in March, 1969,
was as follows:

Sector	Percent
Agriculture	44.6
Modern Economic Infrastructure	33.5
Social Development	21.4
Other	0.5
	100.0

During the ten years in which the first and
second EDFs have operated, they have been empowered
to disburse $1,350 million, largely for Africa. The
EDF is thus the third largest aid disburser for
Africa, after France and Britain. The associated
Afro-Malagasy countries contain 60 million people,
a little more than one-fifth of the population of
Africa. Annual disbursements of the EDF run at the
rate of $45 million per year, which is half the
amount of the British aid program to the whole of
Africa.

Both its size and its method of administering
aid therefore deserve serious study. There are a
number of lessons for other donors to be learned
from the EDF. Among them are the advantages of long-
term forward commitments, the role of overseas representation, the experience of joint undertakings,
the opportunity to spend funds anywhere in twenty-
four countries or even beyond, and the integration
of aid into a package of economic and technical cooperation.[7]

Commitments over five years avoid the uncertainties and wastes of annual wrangles over budgetary
appropriations. The EDF seems to combine some of the
better features of bilateral aid, such as donor's
control, with some of the better features of multilateral aid, such as certainty for the recipient and
less direct political control. Since the Fund is
intended to supplement bilateral and other multilateral
aid, joint ventures with bilateral and multilateral
donors and with private capital are undertaken. In
principle, purchases can be made anywhere in the EEC
or in the eighteen associated states, although in
fact traditional, administrative, and personal links
with France give her a large share of the orders.
The fact that 25 percent of the contracts go to enterprises in the associated states refutes the often-
cited belief that other African countries would not
be able to deliver the goods required for development
projects. (See Chapter 13.) Local project managers
ensure the efficient use of the aid. The men are
technicians and managers from many nations and divorced
from the political taints of diplomats.

The manner in which the EDF selects and finances
projects also has important lessons. The finance
covers total costs of a project, not just foreign
exchange content (like much bilateral aid), but it
covers only projects. The EDF does not provide program aid. In this way, efficient use of funds is
sought and the possibility of corruption is minimized.

Technical assistance and advice is given for
the preparation of dossiers for application for
support.... Among the criteria that are used

in deciding whether or not to give support
are the urgency of the needs to be satisfied,
the likely increment of productivity that
will result from the project when completed,
the extent to which it will contribute to
diversification of the economy, and how big
a role it can play in promoting regional cooperation. The committee wishes to satisfy
itself that the project is being promoted
in an appropriate context of the overall
development plan of the country concerned.
It is precisely at this point that overseas
representatives can be so valuable.[8]

Among its deficiencies are the rule that responsibilities end once a project is completed, so that
project management, one of the greatest needs in
Africa, is excluded; delays between commitments and
disbursements are long, partly because tenders from
twenty-four countries have to be invited. And the
joint operations give rise to complexities of aid coordination as a result of the different financial
procedures and different rules about local cost
financing.

VOLUNTARY AID

Although a thorough discussion of the size and
quality of all forms of nonofficial aid lie outside
the terms of reference of this study, a few words
on voluntary aid may be in order, if only to put its
contribution into perspective. The DAC of the Organization for Economic Cooperation and Development (OECD)
has estimated that total resources handled annually
by nonprofit organizations exceed not $1,000 million.
Of this sum, $700 million is raised by private bodies
and the remainder takes the form of food, clothing,
and other supplies distributed by voluntary agencies
in developing countries. Of the total, Africa receives
about one-third. It is also estimated that about
60,000 persons hold salaried posts in nongovernmental
aid activity, two-thirds of them working in the field.

The main problems arising from the voluntary
effort are whether more effective coordination could

be achieved and whether administrative costs as a
ratio of disbursements can be cut. Attempts are now
being made to achieve some form of coordination, but
it appears that not much has yet been achieved. The
distribution of funds and of technical assistance
continues to be largely haphazard. Each agency relies
on its own overseas contacts and responds to ad hoc
schemes which conform to its own objectives. There
may be a basic conflict between the appeal to voluntary
contributions and efficient coordination. The former
is often based on harnessing enthusiasm for small-
scale and specific objectives, the latter on large-
scale administration and program planning.

The question has also been raised to what extent
time, energy, and funds of these agencies should be
diverted from collecting money and sponsoring projects
to political pressure on governments. In spite of
the size of the total voluntary contribution, in any
particular country a change of government policy often
can wipe out a multiple of the voluntary contributions.

                            NOTES

1. Ministère des Affaires Étrangères, Direction
Générale des Affaires Culturelles et Techniques,
Rapport d'Activités, 1963.

2. The Development Aid Policy of the Federal
Republic of Germany, federal government memorandum
for DAC 1968 annual audit (Bonn: Press and Information Office of the Federal Government, 1968), p. 14.

3. Report of the DAC on the conclusions and
recommendations of the informal meeting of experts
on aid to education in Africa, held on May 29-30,
1969, DAC (69)39.

4. Lester B. Pearson et al., Partners in
Development: Report of the Commission on International Development (New York: Praeger Publishers,
1969) pp. 211, 212.

5. UNCTAD, External Development Finance: Present and Future, TD/B/C.3/61, p. 25.

6. The cost of borrowing on the capital markets has been increasing steadily: from 4.1 percent a year in 1963 to 5.6 percent in 1966 and 5.95 percent in the United States in August, 1967; 6 percent in Sweden in 1967; and 6.54 percent on the New York market in March, 1967-8. As a consequence, the rate of interest on the Bank's loans to developing countries was raised from 5.5 percent a year to 6 percent in February, 1966; to 6.25 percent in January, 1968; and to 6.5 percent in August, 1968. United Nations, The Expternal Financing of Economic Development 1963-67, E/4652. In 1969 the World Bank was charging interest at the rate of 7 percent a year.

7. See Tom Soper, "The European Development Fund and Its Operations with Africa," Journal of Administration Overseas (October, 1968).

8. Ibid., p. 524.

Statistics on capital flows are notoriously bad.
The data rarely show private debts, and even the
statistics for public debt service are incomplete.
The figures for foreign-owned capital are quite
inadequate. We therefore do not know the service
burden of foreign capital. In the nature of things,
we are ignorant about illegal capital flows and
about the distortions of trade flows which should be
attributed to these illegal flows. Effective aid
requires reliable statistics. But the statistics of
aid require aid for statistics. A particularly
valuable form of technical assistance would be the
provision of more statisticians for ministries.
These are often scarce in donor countries, too, and
donor governments may be reluctant to release them.
Yet their value in making the whole planning process
more effective is a multiple of their nominal salaries.
This combined note of warning and plea is put in
early in order to avoid throughout the study, whenever
statistics are used, repeated specific warnings about
their unreliability.

Africa, in addition to sharing in the broadly
adverse trends of total aid (lower proportion of
national income of donors, decline in the real value
as a result of inflation, lower proportion of grants,
rising debt burden, and, for some countries, deteri-
orating export prices), suffered from additional
weaknesses peculiar to the transfer of resources to

TABLE 15

Net Flow of Official Loans and Grants to the Developing
Countries and the Multilateral Agencies 1960-66
(million $)

	1960	1961	1962	1963	1964	1965	1966-*
Latin America	289	768	856	1,097	922	997	1,199
Africa	1,482	1,655	1,777	1,667	1,766	1,707	1,604
Asia and the Pacific	2,316	2,297	2,488	2,861	2,981	3,336	3,356
All Developing Countries	4,225	4,917	5,372	5,918	5,933	6,224	6,425

*Preliminary.

Source: United Nations, The External Financing of Economic Development, 1962-66,

Africa. Africa's share in total aid fell from about
35 percent in 1960 to about 27 percent in 1965 and
to 23 percent in 1967. The comparative figures are
given in Table 15.

In addition to the declining share, aid to Africa
fluctuated more than for other regions. Although
aid in 1966 was larger than in 1960, in three out of
seven years--i.e., in 1963, 1965, and 1966--it was
less than in the preceding year. The volume of aid
to Africa reached its peak in 1962, when it stood at
$1,777 million, or $6.50 per head. By 1966 aid had
declined to $1,604 million, or $5.30 per head. If
the 1966 volume is adjusted for changes in prices of
manufactures entering into international trade, the
$1,604 million at current prices reduce to $1,499
million at 1960 unit value of manufactures.*

Furthermore, it is estimated that between 1960
and 1967 the net flow of investment income out of
Africa more than tripled, from $187 million to $678
million, or from 12.6 percent of net official inflow
to about 42 percent. Data on other forms of legal
and illegal capital outflows are difficult to collect,
but the flow must be substantial.

Africa's share of the flow of net direct private
investment to less developed countries is estimated
to have been 17 percent in 1965. Assuming (quite
arbitrarily) that Africa's share of total net private
flow was 17 percent throughout the decade, Table 16
shows the estimated total net transfer of resources
to Africa from 1960 to 1967.

It will be seen that official and private flows
to Africa from DAC member countries net of amortization, investment income, and interest payments
were smaller in 1966 than in any previous year. They
show a slight rise in 1967 over 1966, but still remain
below the level of any other previous year. Moreover,

---

*United Nations, The External Financing of Econ-
nomic Development 1962-66, E/4438.

TABLE 16

Estimated Total Flow of Resources to Africa, 1960-67
(million $)

	1960	1961	1962	1963	1964	1965	1966	1967
Total Net Official Flow	1,482	1,655	1,777	1,667	1,760	1,707	1,604	1,610
Net Private Flow	507	530	396	438	535	688	673	683
Total Official and Private Flow	1,989	2,185	2,173	2,105	2,295	2,395	2,277	2,293
Net Outflow of Profits, Interest, and Dividends	187	183	202	323	565	624	750	678
Total Official and Private Flows*	1,802	2,002	1,971	1,782	1,730	1,771	1,527	1,615

*Net of amortization and investment income.

Sources: United Nations, External Development Finance 1962-66, 1963-67, OECD, 1968 Review.

the net outflow of profits and interest is understated
because some data are missing. This means, first,
that the net flow of resources to Africa is overstated
and, second, if untraced outflows grew over the period
1960-67, the decline in the transfer of resources to
Africa is understated.

However, the evidence for a decline in the net
transfer of resources to Africa is not conclusive
because we do not have adequate data on private flows
and the resulting reverse flows. What we can say
with some degree of confidence is that the net real
transfer of resources to Africa from the industrialized
countries did not increase over the period 1960-67.

For the period 1967-68 and for twenty-seven
African countries, selected on the basis of availability of data, the evidence for a declining flow is
strong. (See Tables 17 and 18.)

Table 17 shows that for twenty-seven African
countries the receipts of official donations and
long-term capital, net of repayments and repatriation,
fell from $1,161 million in 1967 to $1,025 million
in 1968. Excluding oil-rich Libya, Algeria, and
Nigeria, the decline is not quite so pronounced. At
$792 million in 1968, the receipts of the other
twenty-four countries were about 93 percent of the
1967 level of $854 million. Fifteen of the twenty-
seven countries show lower receipts in 1968 compared
with 1967, while Libya registered a sharp outflow in
1968. For only eleven countries are the receipts
higher than in 1967.

Over the same period, receipts of sixty-seven
developing countries, selected on the basis of
availability of data, net of repayments and repatriation, show a decline of 3 percent. The share of the
twenty-seven African countries in the total flow
declined from 15.7 percent in 1967 to 14.4 percent
in 1968.

Over the same years and for the same group of
African countries the net outflow of interest and
profits increased. Hence the decline in the real

TABLE 17

Selected Developing Countries: Net Receipts of Official Donations and
Long-Term Capital, 1967-68
(million $)

Country	Central Government and Central Monetary Institutions Transfer Payments (net)		Net Change in Long-Term Private Capital[a]		Total Inflow (net)	
	1967	1968	1967	1968	1967	1968
Algeria	51	79	40[b]	40[b]	91	128
Cameroon	36	43	...	...	36	43
Central African Republic	6	5	...	...	6	5
Chad	8	20	...	--[b]	8	20
Congo (Brazzaville)	10	4	10	6	20	10
Congo (Kinshasa)	66	42	-5	-4	61	38
Ethiopia	18	19	10	24	28	43
Gabon	2	4	...	...	2	4
Ghana	21	28	35	14	56	42
Guinea	19	13	-	-	19	13
Ivory Coast	31	51	13	16	44	67
Kenya	35	53	33	35	70	88
Libya	1	2	19	-79	20	-77
Madagascar	50	57	...	...	50	57
Malawi	31	28	10	10	41	38
Mali	27	23	...	...	27	23
Mauritania	12	10	-5	...	7	10
Mauritius	9	6	--	--	9	6

50

Morocco	86	78	9	7	95	85
Nigeria	59	34	137	148	196	182
Senegal	42	10	...	...	42	10
Sierra Leone	5	2	11	9	16	11
Somalia	20	22	2	2	22	24
Sudan	43	14	--	1[b]	43	15
Tanzania	25	29	-10	11	15	40
Togo	12	6	-3	...	9	6
Tunisia	98	76	30	18	128	94
Africa: 27 Countries	823	758	338	267	1161	1025
24 Countries[c]	712	643	142	149	854	782
Latin America: 23 Countries	657	717	1191	1451	1848	2168
Asia: 17 Countries	3606	2987	756	923	4362	3910
Total: 67 Developing Countries	5088	4474	2281	2650	7373	7124
59 Developing Countries	4541	3739	1794	2187	6335	5926

Notes: Positive figures denote grants received or capital inflows; negative figures denote grants extend or capital outflows.

Totals are not always the sum of items given, owing to rounding.

... = not available or separately reported.

-- = nil or negligible.

[a]Including net borrowing by local institutions and private monetary institutions.
[b]Excluding reinvested profits.
[c]Excluding oil-producing Algeria, Libya, and Nigeria.
[d]Other than petroleum exporters (Algeria, Libya, Nigeria, Iran, Iraq, Saudi Arabia, Venezuela, and Trinidad-Tobago).

Source: United Nations, The External Financing of Economic Development 1964-68, E/4815.

TABLE 18

Selected African Countries: Real Net Transfer of Resources, 1967-68
(million $)

	1967	1968
27 Countries		
Net Inflow of Official Donations and Long-Term Capital	1,161	1,025
Net Outflow of Interest and Profits	912	1,120
Net Transfer of Resources	249	-93
24 Countries (excluding Algeria, Libya and Nigeria)		
Net Inflow of Official Donations and Long-Term Capital	854	792
Net Outflow of Interests and Profits	360	421
Net Transfer of Resources	494	371

Source: United Nations, The External Financing of Economic Development, 1964-68, E/4851.

net transfer of resources was even steeper.   (See
Table 18.)

An inflow of $249 million in 1967 had turned
into an outflow of $93 million in 1968.   However, if
we exclude Algeria, Libya, and Nigeria, the remaining
countries, as a group, show a positive net transfer
of resources in 1968, although well below that of
1967.   The net inflow of this latter group fell from
$494 million in 1967 to $371 million in 1968 as a
result of declining receipts of official donations
and long-term capital, on the one hand, and a larger
outflow of interests and profits, on the other.   The
latter is common to all developing countries; the
former is peculiar to Africa.

In addition, for a full assessment of the aid
contribution, allowance must be made for several
other factors:

1.   As a result of the rising prices of manufactured imports and the fall in the prices of some
commodity exports, the terms of trade of many African
countries have deteriorated, the import capacity of
the exports earnings has fallen, and the real value
of a given money quantum of aid has dropped.

2.   There is likely to have been a growing
capital flow out of Africa, although this is difficult
to prove.

3.   As a result of increased tying and harder
terms, the real value of the aid has fallen.

4.   Since developed countries have continued to
grow, the percentage of their national income devoted
to aid to Africa has fallen considerably.

5.   Finally, as a result of population growth
in Africa, the amount of aid received per head has
dropped.

3

THE

AID

TARGET

In 1967 total net financing flows of DAC members amounted to $11.3 billion, of which Africa received $2.29 billion.* One percent of net national income (NNI) at factor cost would have been $12.1 billion, of which Africa would have received $2.46 billion, had there been a proportional allocation of the additional funds. One percent of gross national product (GNP) at market price would have been $15.1 billion, of which Africa would have received $3.1 billion. Net official aid from DAC members and multilateral agencies ran between 1964 and 1967 at an annual average of $5,680 million, of which Africa received $1,542 million.

On the assumption that OECD member countries' combined GNP would rise at an annual rate of 4.3 percent (at constant prices) over the decade ending in 1975, the volume of net assistance would have to increase by 90 percent between 1967 and 1975, or 8 percent per year at constant prices, if the 1 percent target was to be reached in that year. The projection for 1975 is $17.0 billion as 1 percent of NNI, about the same if the target of net official DAC aid is 0.7 percent of gross national product, and $21.2

---

*Total net official flow plus estimated net private flow.

billion as 1 percent of GNP.*   In additoin, in order
to achieve this net flow, the gross flow will have
to increase even more, in order to allow for amortization payments.

Assuming Africa's share in the 1975 flow to be
about the same as it was in 1967, the projected net
flow (at present prices) would be about $4 billion.
But the 1967 share in total aid represents a sharp
decline from Africa's share in earlier years. Africa's
share in the net flow of multilateral and official
bilateral finance from DAC countries had fallen from
about 33 percent in 1960 to about 26 percent in 1965
and 23 percent in 1967**. If the 1960 share were to
be restored in 1975, Africa's share would then be
about $5.6 billion.

Assuming that world net official aid is increased
by 1975 to the 1 percent of the NNI target from the
present $7 billion to $17 billion and that Africa's
share remains constant, so that Africa would receive
between $4 billion and $5 billion, the question
arises whether, and how best, such a large increase
could be spent. We have serious doubts about the
usefulness of the notion of limited absorptive
capacity (see Chapter 10) and draw attention to the
need to support capital aid with the right forms of
technical assistance, and in particular project
selection, preparation, execution, and management,
in order to make use effectively of rising amounts.
But the question remains as to what would be the best
channels and forms which such an increased aid flow
should take.

As far as multilateral aid is concerned, the
problem is discussed in the section of United Nations

---

*Development Assistance Efforts and Policies,
1968 Review.

**Calculated from OECD, Geographical Distribution
of Financial Flows to Less Developed Countries,
1960-64, 1965, 1966-67 (Paris: Organization for Economic Cooperation, 1968).

capacity and attention is drawn to the need for
improved recruitment and training of United Nations
personnel and to the need for reorganizing the lines
of responsibility and the division of duties of the
specialized agencies and the UNDP.

The first priority should be to feed those
already existing institutions which are starved for
funds. Foremost among these is the ADB. It has the
capacity to disburse additional capital. It can
draw on detailed, local knowledge, either directly
or indirectly by supporting local or subregional
development companies, and it can encourage subregional,
multinational projects and thus help to overcome the
market limitations from which many purely national
projects suffer. It can carry out the coordination
of different donors' aid, and it might even move into
managing, as well as financing, projects. Here lies
a rich potential source of the effective use of extra
aid. Although its charter precludes the Bank itself
from receiving funds from non-African countries,
there is a provision in the charter for the establishment of special funds which non-African countries
can join. It is in accordance with this provision
that the Bank has proposed the establishment to the
African Development Fund.

Africa, even more than other regions, needs a
strong regional development bank with external
sources of finance, partly because of the greater
need for regional cooperation and integration and
partly because of the existence of so many small and
poor countries with national incomes below, say,
$2 billion.

The Pearson Commission matched the 1 percent
aid target for donors with a 6 percent annual growth
target for recipients. The analysis is usually
conducted in terms of the "gap" between investment
requirements and domestic savings, or between foreign
exchange requirements and export earnings. We shall
argue later that the gap approach, for a number of
reasons, is inadequate and misleading in identifying
the specific contributions that foreign assistance
can make to accelerated African development. But if,

for tactical purposes, a gap approach to foreign
assistance was adopted, it could be shown that the
target set by the Pearson Commission of 6 percent
annual growth for the 1970's, if applied to Africa,
could be hit only by a substantial increase in aid,
approximately a doubling by 1975.

In order to nearly double aggregate annual growth
rates from 3.3 percent (1965-68 annual average) to
6 percent, and on the assumption of constant capital/
output ratios, development expenditures would have
to be nearly doubled. Assuming the same ratios
between domestic and foreign contributions (now 1/4-
1/3) or between imports and foreign assistance (now
over 1/4) to continue, aid contributions on soft
terms and at constant prices would also have to be
nearly doubled. If the aim were to reduce the ratio
of foreign to domestic contributions, or of foreign
assistance to imports, from their present rather
high values (24 percent and 28 percent, respectively),
correspondingly less would be required. A falling
capital/output ratio would also reduce requirements.
To this must be added service on past debt. Even
on optimistic assumptions, a gap approach would
suggest foreign assistance requirements of nearly
$4 billion at constant prices and on concessional
terms in 1975. Whether we consider the 1 percent
aid target or the 6 percent growth target, we reach
roughly the same figure of $4 billion for 1975.
There is no doubt that, given the right quality and
type of assistance, no difficulties in absorbing
this amount need arise.

It must, however, be emphasized that in addition
to the general dificiencies of gap estimates of aid
requirements, in the case of Africa quality and
composition are of particular importance. The required
changes are discussed at various places throughout
this study. The institutional changes required of
multilateral agencies; the need for a multinational,
subregional approach; and the emphasis on project
preparation and execution and, above all, on concessional terms, all point in the direction of the
creation of a strong African Development Fund,
administered by the ADB drawing on the expertise of
the ECA.

4

WHAT
SHOULD BE COUNTED
AS AID?

Official economic development aid is a payment from one government to another, on concessionary terms, to promote economic development or to prevent economic decline. Three types of payment should be clearly distinguished from aid, because if they are aid at all, they can be regarded as aid, not to a developing country, but only to a group of citizens in the donor country:

1. Compensation for former colonial civil servants;

2. Compensation payments for expatriate farmers (e.g., in the white highlands of Kenya) or owners of mineral rights (e.g., the British South Africa Company in Zambia);

3. Refinance credit to make it possible to repay commercial export credits.

Preindependence commitments, such as pensions for former colonial civil servants and for their widows and orphans, should be fully taken over by the former colonial power and should not be counted as aid. The reason is only partly semantic; the main reason is moral and political. To count such payments as "aid," whatever the declarations made on independence, appears as an attempt to disguise clear

responsibilities to donors' own citizens incurred
when they were recruited by and were answerable to
Britain. This impression can spread to other, genuine
forms of aid and smudge the image of genuine aid
efforts. It has also poisoned the relations between
Great Britain and Tanzania.

The suggestion is that the DAC should provide a
definition of aid excluding these and similar transactions (e.g., the reparation payments of Germany
and Japan). The DAC does not define aid, but at
present it is customary for member countries to claim
all "transfers" of resources (with maturities of over
five years), including private overseas investment
(although this is shown separately). Much can be
gained by a clearer separation of genuine development
aid from funds paid out for other reasons.

It could be argued, on the other side, that
financial relief from any obligations which might
otherwise have constituted a claim on the foreign
exchange earnings and reserves of African countries
may, indirectly, contribute to development. Even
commercial debt relief, where otherwise default would
have occurred, contributes to the credit standing of
the debtor and hence to his ability to raise development finance. On the other hand, countries have
defaulted and nationalized without adequate compensation, and yet continued to receive aid. The economic
case for exclusion of the above items from aid finances,
though strong, is not clinching. It would be difficult to get all DAC members to agree on a definition
of aid. A reasonable interim objective would be to
get a more detailed classification of "transfers" in
DAC statistics, so as to gain a clearer picture of
the direct development assistance rendered.

The British government made loans to countries
achieving independence so that they could pay pensions
to former colonial civil servants, and these countries
made solemn declarations to honor these loans. If
all payments of pensions to former British colonial
officers were taken over by the British government,
the total sum would be £12 to £14 million per year.
This obligation has now, in principle, been taken

over by the British government. It should be deducted
from the aid program, and compensating increases of
genuine development aid should be made. Even if
compensating increases were ruled out, it does not
follow that the cuts should be in aid to precisely
those countries which now carry the responsibility
for the pension payments. (Some of these, like Hong
Kong, do not receive any aid.) Given the existence
of an aid ceiling and given the propriety for Britain
to accept financial responsibility for all pensions,
the consequent cuts, if they have to be made, should
occur in the areas of lowest development priorities.

A special problem is presented to that group of
developing countries which is at an early stage of
development, a group to which many African countries
belong, by suppliers' credits, which are used to
promote exports of equipment, are often but not
always guaranteed by a government agency, and are
extended at high interest rates for short or medium
terms. When the day of reckoning comes, they cannot
always be repaid, and refinancing becomes necessary.
Such refinancing involves concerted action among all
creditors, lest any one creditor fear that his
concession merely goes to service the loans of the
others. The refinancing operations channel aid
resources not necessarily to those who need them most
or manage their affairs best, and provide no incentives for greater caution in the future. It is for
these reasons that restrictions on this type of credit
should be imposed jointly by creditor-exporters and,
if possible, by debtor-importers. The goods bought
with these credits often do not have a high development priority, and the exercise of renegotiating
debts that cannot be repaid does not contribute to
fruitful international cooperation or even to credit-
worthiness. This is not to deny that there is a place
for short- and medium- term commercial credits; but
their amount, their proportion to other debt, and
their place in the development efforts--not the
pressures of the export lobbies of industrial coun-
tries--should be carefully considered. And there is
no case at all for calling them "aid."

FORMS OF AID

Much of the debate on aid has in the past been conducted in terms of contrasts, such as multilateral versus bilateral aid; project versus program aid; commodity aid versus cash aid; capital aid versus technical assistance; official aid versus private foreign investment; aid versus trade, etc. Proponents of each have mustered arguments to bolster up their case. This kind of debate has suffered from three fundamental flaws.

In the first place, much of the debate has been conducted without a clear specification of objectives. There is little point in emphasizing one or the other form of aid--or, indeed, forms of nonaid--without a clear view as to which aim or aims are deemed to be more effectively served by such emphasis. One result of this confusion of aims has been a swing between policies, motivated by disappointments attributable to the question.

Second, most of the policies contrasted contain more than one dimension of activity; and it is not only possible, but often desirable (in the light of certain specified objectives), to combine some features of one with other features of the other. Thus the more successful consultative groups or the EDF has succeeded in combining certain features of multi-lateralism with others of bilateralism. Projects selected in the context and in support of a develop-ment program combine the virtues of control peculiar to project aid with the virtues of backing appropriate policies, characteristic of program aid. Limited reciprocal untying combines some of the virtues of untied aid with some of the advantages to donors of tying.

Third, certain features of the forms of aid contrasted are complementary to one another: physical and social overheads, financed by official aid, make it possible for private investment to operate more profitably; soft-term loans make it possible to service hard loans and high-return investment; only a

well-worked-out program can provide the framework for
useful projects; capital aid can be more effectively
utilized if it is accompanied by technical assistance.
What appear at first sight as alternatives often turn
out to be, on closer inspection, complements.

An important area in which aid could be used
most effectively to stimulate trade is aid for export
credits of developing countries. It is not enough
to produce and sell exports if short-term credits
cannot be extended to finance these exports. A scheme
by which advanced countries provide finance for the
exports of developing countries could make a contribution toward overcoming one important obstacle to
the promotion of larger exports from developing
African countries.

The conclusion is that the starting point should
be aims and objectives; policies should then be derived
from these, rather than be dictated by doctrinal
priorities in abstracto.

THE WORLD FOOD PROGRAM

The World Food Program is a joint UN/FAO multilateral program which provides largely food aid to
promote economic and social development through pilot
projects and also provides emergency relief. Its
disbursements have grown from $3 million in 1962 to
$46 million in 1968 and are projected to grow to
$266 million in 1976.* Of 357 development projects
in 1969, costing a total of $650 million, Mediterranean
Europe, the Near East, and Africa accounted for 216
projects at a total cost of $430 million. Of eighty-
nine emergency operations at a total cost of $65
million the same region accounted for fifty-six
projects at a total cost of $33 million. The program

---

*Food Aid and Related Issues During the Second
Development Decade, Report of the Intergovernmental
Committee on the World Food Program WFP/IGC 17/5
Rev. 1 (April 15, 1970).

attempts to ensure that food aid does not have harmful
effects on the agriculture of developing countries
and on normal commercial trade. Future scope may lie
in the opportunities to buy food surpluses produced
in developing countries with cash contributions from
developed countries and using them, with proper safeguards, for development and relief.

The African Development Fund might support a
food program in conjunction with the World Food Program. The aim would be to use surpluses from one
region; finance storage, transport, and marketing,
and channel the surpluses into areas deficient in
food. Particular care would have to be taken to
combine this with encouragements to local food
production.

5

**AID
PRIORITIES
FOR
AFRICA**

While an effective aid package must combine capital and technical assistance of the right kinds and
must not be offset by canceling policies for trade
and private capital flows, one overriding priority
can be singled out for African countries: technical
assistance, particularly technical assistance which
enables recipients to make the fullest and best use
of whatever other forms of aid are offered and of
their own local resources. Technical assistance in
1967 constituted nearly 40 percent of all aid disbursements to Africa. A good deal of current talk
about "the failure of aid," "lack of absorptive capacity," and "waste" amounts to not much more than
saying that certain forms of technical assistance
have been absent or inadequate or improperly administered or wrongly chosen, and have thus prevented
recipients from making better use of a larger volume
of capital aid.

In particular, technical assistance is needed
to negotiate and disburse loans speedily and effi-
ciently. There is a curious asymmetry in many donors'
assumption that African recipients are underdeveloped
and in need of development aid while, at the same
time, their negotiating machinery is assumed to be
highly developed and efficient.

Another sphere where more technical assistance
would be useful is that of project preparation,

feasibility studies, and preinvestment surveys.
Some of this would be part of an attempt to strengthen
the negotiating machinery, because aid requests pre-
suppose properly prepared projects. But the assistance
would apply also to nonaid projects and thus enable
recipients to make better use of their own resources
in both the public and the private sectors.

A third area of technical assistance would be
with efficient management of projects after they
have been completed. At present, too many projects
are handed over at a stage when assistance in ensuring
efficient use becomes most important. The emphasis
on capital aid, as distinct from aid to recurrent
expenditure, has distorted aid efforts away from assistance to the most efficient utilization of machinery
and equipment and has led to some waste.

The principal need in this area is for enterprise
and management to identify, execute, and initially
run projects, and gradually to hand over ownership,
management, and jobs. Such transfers require an
exercise of the institutional imagination, for present
forms of enterprise and organization do not precisely
meet these needs. Private foreign enterprise, on
the one hand, is interested in profits and not directly
in training local labor, developing local ownership,
and stimulating local entrepreneurship. Official
assistance, on the other hand, tends to confine itself
to financing the project and putting it on the ground,
without showing a continuing interest in its efficient
management and success. The Commonwealth Development
Corporation, possibly unique among development institutions, attempts to bridge this gap by combining
finance, know-how, management, and "Africanization."
It also acts as a catalyst in mobilizing other agents,
be they private or public, domestic or foreign. If
ideological objections of various kinds can be overcome, there is a good deal of scope for evolving
new forms of institutions, particularly adapted for
African countries. Their purpose would be to use
official funds to start enterprises and remedy the
initial shortage of entrepreneurial talent, with a
brief to sell out gradually and to use the funds
thus liberated to start a new project.

A good deal of attention has been paid to improving the quality of financial assistance, much
less, to making technical assistance more effective.
It is not enough to provide "experts" to carry out
certain assignments. The experts' contribution has
to be integrated into the whole complex development
effort and must activate the latent indigenous resources. Far too much technical assistance never
"takes root" and simply reinforces the enclave nature
of so much foreign investment and even foreign aid.
A more careful planning of the aims of technical
assistance, the recruitment and training of experts,
and evaluation of their contribution and of their
impact on the economy and society are necessary.
Neither counting sums of money nor counting numbers
of experts is a very relevant exercise in such a
review of the quality of technical assistance.

Another priority area is the need to encourage
agriculture for domestic consumption. Aid to agriculture suffers from the following difficulties:

1. The technical knowledge available from advanced industrial countries is often inappropriate.
Local knowledge and research are needed, as the new
seeds have demonstrated.

2. The returns, unlike those on industrial
projects, are widely dispersed; and the aid loans
should therefore be on considerably softer terms.

3. The channeling of aid should make much greater
use of those who know local conditions where direct
intergovernmental lending is inappropriate. Thought
should be given to the most appropriate channels. One
way may be contributions to local agricultural finance
or development corporations. Another way would be
to relieve local budgets of certain obligations
which could just as well be financed by aid, such
as the maintenance of roads, thereby freeing local
budgetary resources for finance agricultural schemes.

4. Agricultural schemes, to be successful,
require a number of complementary and supporting
activities: irrigation, credit, transport, extension

services, storage, etc. In addition, since the masses
of the poorest people live and work on the land, social
objectives must be borne in mind when agricultural
reform is carried out. The nucleus estate, providing
extension services and marketing facilities and all
the virtues of the most up-to-date modern enterprise,
round which cluster a group of smallholders, provides
one pattern of agricultural development worth ex-
tending.

AFRICA'S DEBT

The experience of the World Bank in 1967 illus-
trates the kind of situation which could develop over
time if multilateral hard-term lending by the regional
development banks and others increases without a
simultaneous rise in soft loans and grants. Although
gross disbursements of the IBRD to Africa, Asia, and
Latin America rose in 1967 to $510 million, a 22
percent increase over the average level of the previous
three years, disbursements net of amortization fell
by $10 million. To maintain disbursements net of
repayments constant, an increase of 25 percent in
gross disbursements would have been necessary. To
attain an expansion of, say, 15 percent, an increase
in gross disbursements of over 35 percent would have
been required in 1967.[1]

It should be noted that payments of interest on
multilateral lending have not been taken into account.
If they were, the actual transfer of resources to
less developed countries from the multilateral agencies
would of course be seen to be much less. For example,
gross disbursements by the World Bank group amounted
to about $870 million in 1967, whereas disbursements
net of amortization, subscriptions, and contributions,
and of changes in holdings in developing countries
of the funded debt of the IBRD, amounted to $545
million. Interest received by the World Bank group

69

amounted to over $200 million in 1967 (23 percent of
gross disbursements). Thus the real net transfer of
resources amounted only to $345 million, or about 40
percent of gross disbursements.[2]

The tendency to focus attention on gross flows
of capital or on flows that are net only of amortization and capital repatriation is thus liable to obscure
the important question of how much foreign resources
contribute to the capacity of the developing countries
to import. It has been estimated that approximately
half of the gross flow to developing countries is
offset by amortization, interest, and dividend payments
and that the gross flow will continue to be offset
by these payments at an accelerating rate if present
terms continue.[3]

The outstanding external public debt of ninety-
seven less developed countries rose from $10 billion
in 1956 to over $39 billion in 1965. The estimated
service payments on external public debt rose from
less than $0.8 billion to $3.5 billion, nearly half
of which was attributable to export credits.[4]

For eighty-one developing countries external
public debt outstanding increased by 38 percent over
the period 1965-68, from $37.78 billion to $53.36
billion. During the same period estimated payments
of interest and amortization also increased by about
38 percent, to $4.67 billion in 1968. Of these eighty-
one countries, thirty-eight are African; and their
external indebtedness increased from $6.28 billion
in 1965 to $8.72 billion at the end of 1968. Table
16 also shows that their service payments rose sharply,
from $0.47 billion in 1965 to $0.63 billion in 1968.

The World Bank data do not include figures for
unguaranteed export credits, debt repayable at the
option of the borrower in local currencies, or commercial arrears. "If we further take into account the
possibility that even the data on public and publicly
guaranteed debt may be understated to some extent,
the total outstanding debt of the developing countries
could well have exceeded $45 billion at the end of
the year 1966 and debt service could have amounted
to more than $5 billion."[5] The World Bank estimates

TABLE 19

External Public Debt Outstanding and Debt Service Payments, 1961-68
(billion dollars; end of period)

			Total[a]	Africa[b]
Debt Outstanding	1961		21.59	3.31
	1962		25.94	4.04
	1963		29.71	4.97
	1964		33.17	5.52
	1965		37.78	6.28
	1966		42.70	7.35
	1967		47.93	8.06
	1968	Total	53.36	8.72
		Disbursed	39.96	6.94
		Undisbursed	13.41	1.78
Service Payments	1961		2.31	0.17
	1962		2.58	0.22
	1963		2.75	0.49
	1964		3.18	0.43
	1965		3.39	0.47
	1966		3.90	0.47
	1967		4.16	0.47
	1968		4.67	0.63

[a]1961-64, 79 countries; 1965-68, 81 countries.
[b]1961-64, excluding Mauritius.

Source: World Bank/IDA, Annual Report (1969, 1970).

71

outstanding public debt of developing countries to
be $41 billion in 1966.

Consequently the debt service ratio (amortization
and interest as a proportion of commodity export
earnings) of developing countries rose from less than
4 percent in the mid-1950's to 9 percent in 1965.[6]
The value of the merchandise exports of all LDCs at
about $39 billion in 1965,[7] almost equalled their
external outstanding public debt in that year, as
estimated by the World Bank.

The 1965 regional breakdown of external debt is
estimated to be as follows. Total outstanding unguaranteed suppliers' credits at $1.6 billion, divided
as follows:[8]

Latin America	$0.6 billion
Asia and the Middle East	$0.4 billion
Africa	$0.4 billion
Southern Europe	$0.2 billion

Total reported debt of $39.2 billion is divided
as follows:

Latin America	$11.7 billion
Asia and the Middle East	$16.5 billion
Africa	$6.9 billion
Southern Europe	$4.1 billion

Total reported debt (disbursed) was estimated
at $28.2 billion, which was divided as follows:

Latin America	$9.9 billion
Asia and the Middle East	$10.7 billion
Africa	$4.7 billion
Southern Europe	$2.9 billion

The total of reported debt and outstanding unguaranteed suppliers' credits of Africa thus amounted to
$7.3 billion in 1965. This works out at approximately
$26 per head. The World Bank estimates that Africa's
service payments amounted to $0.63 billion in 1968.
This represents a debt service ratio of 7.2 percent.
The debt service per head was about $2.20. However,

since heavy borrowing is a relatively recent phenomenon
for Africa, growth of debt service is expected to be
faster for Africa than for any other region. The
rate of growth of Africa's debt service payments
between 1960 and 1968 was faster than for any other
region. Over the same period the debt service ratio
increased from somewhat more than 2 percent in 1960
to over 7 percent in 1968.[9] The debt service ratio
of 7 percent takes into account only service payments
on reported outstanding public debt, excluding outflows
associated with unguaranteed suppliers' credits,
private foreign investment, military assistance loans,
and unreported debt.

The outlook for debt service is alarming, unless
measures are taken to soften considerably the terms
of new lending and to convert (reschedule or refinance)
past loans into grants or loans on soft terms.

SOME GENERAL CONSIDERATIONS

Although the literature on the burden of the
debt service in developing countries is mounting, it
is worth stepping back for a moment in order to ask
what the "burden of development debt" is. A hostile
critic may say that any debtor who talks of a "burden"
when it comes to the obligation of repaying his debt
deserves little sympathy. In what sense, if any, can
debt service then be regarded as a burden? If the
yield of a loan exceeds the interest rate and amortization, there remains a net benefit to the borrower;
if not, there is no case for borrowing. This is how
a prudent debtor would look at the problem. The
analogy from the individual domestic borrower is,
however, misleading. In international lending, the
payment of interest and amortization must be effected
by the generation of a surplus of exports over imports.
This so-called "transfer burden" of the debt service
may be (theoretically) positive or negative, depending,
among other things, upon the trade policies pursued
by the remitting and receiving countries. To give
only one illustration of a negative burden, if the
borrower pays interest and principal by raising the
prices of his export commodities in the face of an

inelastic foreign demand, he will be able to purchase the same volume of foreign exchange for fewer exports.

The "problem of debt service" arises because there are three distinct hurdles to be overcome by the borrower and several conditions to be fulfilled by the lender. While it is true that a loan normally supplements investment and other development resources and contributes to accelerated capital formation and growth, this growth may, in some conditions be less than the effective cost of the loan if full allowance is made for tying, for repayment in convertible currency, and for the secondary effects of servicing the loan on the terms of trade. Even if the total domestic returns exceed the cost of the loan, the service payments have to be collected in taxes, and the inadequate administrative machinery of African developing countries is not always able to cope with this fiscal requirement. Even if domestic returns, properly calculated, are adequate, and even if the fiscal conditions are fulfilled, the service payments have to be remitted through the balance of payments by stepping up exports or by saving on imports.

The conditions that have to be met by the lender are readiness, in spite of existing indebtedness, to continue to finance development where the fructification period of the investment is long and willingness to accept payment by granting freer access to domestic markets when service payments fall due. It will be seen that it is rare that these conditions are fulfilled. Hence it is legitimate to speak of an international debt problem, even though we should have no sympathy with a domestic borrower who complained about a "burden" when interest and repayment are demanded.

The mounting external debt burden of the developing countries brings out the need for soft loan terms. Furthermore, if development loans are made on soft terms rather than hard, the job of development will be finished sooner and donors will have to furnish less total aid in order to achieve firm development objectives.

This follows from the fact that, as loan terms harden, the net flow of resources decreases. And a decrease in the net flow of resources has two effects: it lengthens the time necessary to do a given job of development, and it increases the amount of aid required to do that job.

This is illustrated by Charts A, B and C, taken from an Agency for International Development (AID) study which brings out clearly the relationships between loan terms and aid requirements. The charts compare the effect of making loans on the following terms:

1. IDA: 0.75 percent interest, fifty years maturity, including a ten-year grace period;

2. AID Minimum: 2 percent interest, forty years maturity, including a ten-year grace period with 1 percent interest;

3. AID Medium: 3.5 percent, twenty years maturity, including a three-year grace period;

4. Hard:* 5.5 percent, thirteen years maturity, including a three-year grace period.

Chart 1 assumes a steady level of lending at the rate of $100 per year. It shows that the net flow will vary substantially, depending upon the loan terms that are used. The harder the terms, the less the net flow. After the eighth year there is no net flow on loans made on hard terms--annual debt service charges exceed the $100 aid level.

Chart 2 compares the gross cost of maintaining a continued net flow of $100 on various loan terms.

———————————————

*These terms are generally in line with those extended by the World Bank, the Export-Import Bank, and others. International lending now takes place on even harder terms, but the study was conducted some time ago.

As loan terms harden, debt service charges mount and
more aid must be provided each year to maintain the
same net flow. For example, to produce $100 of net
flow in the tenth year, $270 of gross aid is required
on hard terms, $195 on AID medium terms, $115 on AID
minimum terms, and $109 on IDA terms.

Chart 3 assumes that the development objective
of a given country can be achieved with an annual
net flow of $100 over a ten-year period and that the
country's repayment capacity will improve fairly
rapidly thereafter. The chart shows that in order
to achieve this objective on IDA terms, gross aid of
$1,040 will have to be provided over a period of 11
years. On AID minimum terms a total of $4,475 will
be required over forty-five years. The additional
amounts over $1,000 are the extra assistance needed
to cover debt servicing until the country's repayment
capacity can do the job. Finally, the chart shows
that the cost of trying to achieve development on
hard terms is clearly excessive--if, indeed, it can
be achieved at all.

Chart 4 shows debt service as a percent of
exports on various assumptions.

Various debt service projections for the period
1966-75 have been made by the United Nations Commission
on Trade and Development secretariat.[10] The interest
and amortization payment falling due from 1966 to
1975 have two components: payments on the initial
debt outstanding on January 1, 1966, and service
payment on new loans contracted during the projection
period itself. The time profile of service payments
on new gross inflows of grants and loans for the
years 1966-75 would depend on the volume of such
inflows, as well as their composition and terms.

By 1975, debt servicing is expected to preempt
23 percent of the export earnings (excluding petroleum
exports) of all less developed countries, on the
following assumptions: (1) terms and composition
of new gross inflows would be the same as in 1965;
(2) net inflow of grants and loans were maintained
at the 1965 level;   (3) export credits grow at 5

CHART 1

Harder Terms Mean Less Real Impact
for each Dollar of Assistance

DECLINE IN NET FLOW OF RESOURCES
IF GROSS LENDING IS MAINTAINED
AT A FIXED LEVEL OF $100 PER YEAR

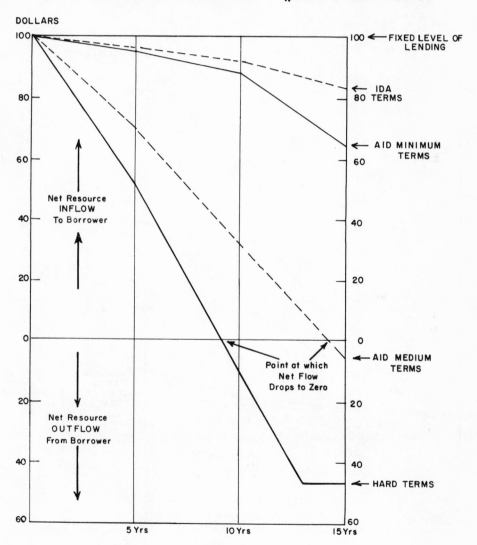

Source: An AID study on debt.

77

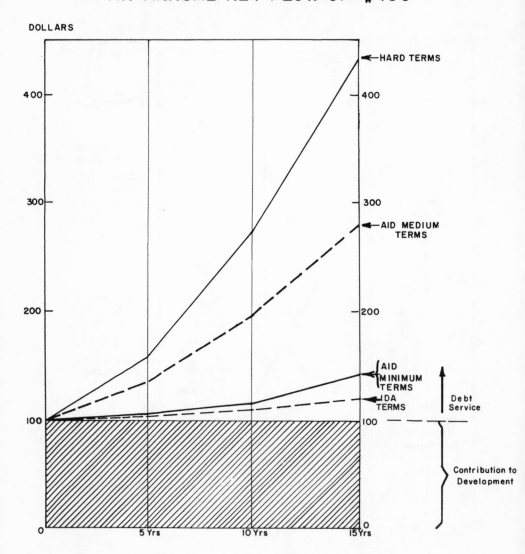

CHART 2

**Harder Terms Mean That More Aid
is Needed to Do The Same Job**

GROSS LENDING PER YEAR
REQUIRED TO MAINTAIN
AN ANNUAL NET FLOW OF $100

DOLLARS

←HARD TERMS

400 — 400

300 — 300

←AID MEDIUM
TERMS

200 — 200

{AID
MINIMUM
TERMS
←IDA
TERMS

Debt
Service

100 — 100

Contribution to
Development

0 — 5 Yrs — 10 Yrs — 15 Yrs — 0

Source: An AID study on debt.

78

CHART 3

Harder Terms Mean Substantially Longer and Larger Assistance Programs

GROSS AID REQUIRED
TO FINANCE $100 OF NET FLOW
FOR 10 YEARS

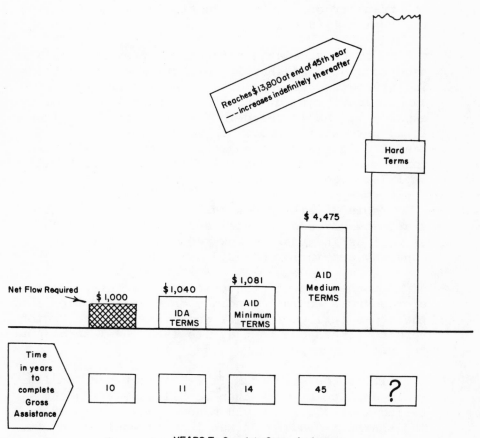

Reaches $13,800 at end of 45th year --increases indefinitely thereafter

Hard Terms

$4,475 — AID Medium TERMS

$1,081 — AID Minimum TERMS

$1,040 — IDA TERMS

Net Flow Required → $1,000

Time in years to complete Gross Assistance

| 10 | 11 | 14 | 45 | ? |

YEARS To Complete Gross Assistance

Note: Assumes moderately rapid improvement in debt servicing capacity after the ten years of net flow.

Source: An AID study in debt.

79

percent per annum; and (4) exports grow at an average of 4 percent per annum.

It can be seen from Table 20 that, for each region, debt service as a percentage of gross inflow is projected to rise considerably from 1966 to 1975. The largest increase occurs for the countries of Africa, where the figure doubles from 26 percent in 1966 to 53 percent in 1975. (This should be seen in the context of our estimate in the study that the net transfer of resources to Africa declined during the period 1960-66.)

Debt service as a percentage of exports is also seen to rise most sharply for Africa, from 11 percent in 1966 to 25 percent in 1975, at a 4 percent per annum growth rate of exports. (Including petroleum exporters, the increase is from 10 percent in 1966 to 22 percent in 1975.) In volume terms, this means that the debt service payments of Africa will more than triple from $0.8 billion in 1966 to $2.6 billion in 1975. (See Table 20.)

Table 20 also shows that Africa registers the sharpest increase in total debt service payments, as well as in gross inflow required to maintain a constant net inflow of $2.3 billion.

Another set of projections shows the net inflow of resources and net lending, on the assumption that the gross inflow of grants and loans to each region were to remain constant at its 1965 level throughout the projection period.

It can be seen from Table 21 that net lending would decline by more than $2 billion during the period 1966-75, and would become negative in 1970. The sharpest decline in net lending would occur for Africa, becoming negative in 1970 at -$0.1 billion and decreasing by another $100 million between 1970 and 1975.

For some of the less developed countries the debt servicing burden reached such proportions as to necessitate rescheduling of debt. The projections

CHART 4

DEBT SERVICE AS PER CENT OF EXPORTS UNDER
ALTERNATIVE ASSUMPTIONS

Assumption A: Exports Grow 5% p.a.

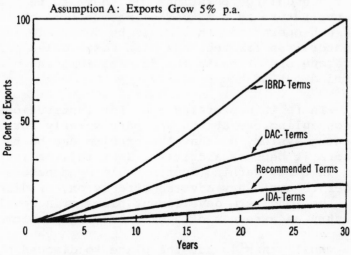

Assumption B: Exports Grow 8% p.a.

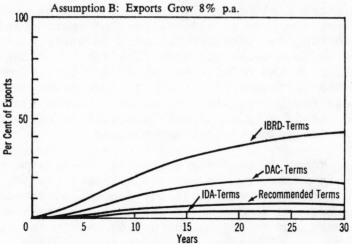

Explanation of terms:	Interest	Maturity	Grace Period
IBRD	7%	25 years	5 years
DAC	3%	25	5
IDA	0.75%	50	10
Recommended Terms	2%	40	10

Note: The net flow of external lending is assumed to be 40% of exports in year zero, increasing by about 2% per annum up to year 15, and then remaining unchanged.

Source : Pearson et al., Partners in
            Development, P. 161.

for debt servicing indicate that an increasing number
of rescheduling operations will have to be launched
in the future as a matter of necessity; the number
of such operations that would be desirable is even
greater. So far debt has been rescheduled only as
a rescue operation in the face of imminent disaster,
carried out <u>ad hoc</u>.

There is a pressing need for institutionalizing
rescheduling operations and particularly for an early
warning system, so that the problem can be tackled
before it becomes a crisis. Institutionalization
and an early warning system would seem necessary in
order to avoid any adverse effects on, or disruption
of, the long-term development plans of a developing
country as a result of debt servicing problems.

While this is not the place to discuss changes
in borrowers' policies, except insofar as they may
affect the flow of aid, fuller information and proper
budgeting for debt service with an early warning
system is a necessary condition for a rational presentation of the problem to donors and for improved relations with donors. Each country should have a
clear and up-to-date picture of its debt situation
and should attempt to make projections of future
liabilities on various assumptions.

There is need for a general overhauling of aid-
giving machinery, in particular for a greater coordination between different donors, on the one hand,
and between donors and recipients, on the other. A
primary aim should be the avoidance, in the first
place, of situations demanding rescheduling. Another
important objective is to stabilize the flow of aid
and reduce uncertainty as to amount of aid in the
future and for a correct assessment of needs and
priorities. All this can best be done within the
perspective of a country's long-term development
plan and potential.

The mounting debt problem is now recognized to
present serious difficulties for aid recipients.
On the other hand, budgetary appropriations for aid
present many donors with difficulties. The following

TABLE 20

Developing Regions: Projected Estimate of Gross Capital Inflow and Debt
Service, 1966-75, Corresponding to a Constant Net Inflow of Resources
(billion $)

	Africa			Asia,			Middle East			Latin America			Total[b]		
	1966	1970	1975	1966	1970	1975	1966	1970	1975	1966	1970	1975	1966	1970	1975
Net Capital Inflow[a]	2.3	2.3	2.3	3.5	3.5	3.5	0.5	0.5	0.5	0.8	0.8	0.8	7.1	7.1	7.1
Gross Capital Inflow	3.1	4.1	4.9	4.9	6.0	6.7	1.2	1.5	1.9	3.0	3.3	4.0	12.2	14.9	17.5
Total Debt Service	0.8	1.7	2.6	1.4	2.5	3.2	0.7	1.0	1.4	2.3	2.5	3.2	5.1	7.8	10.4
Debt Service as Percent of Gross Capital Inflow	26	43	53	29	41	48	58	67	74	75	77	81	42	52	60
Debt Service as Percent of Exports, Assuming Exports Grow at 4 Percent Annually[c]	11	20	25	12	18	19	9	11	12	23	21	22	16	21	23

Note: The net inflow of resources is held constant at the 1965 level and the composition and terms of
net inflow are assumed to be the same as during 1965, except that supplier's credits are assumed to grow at
an annual rate of 5 percent.

[a] Grants and lending net of amortization and interest payments.
[b] Including European developing countries.
[c] Excluding petroleum exporters.

Source: UNCTAD, Growth, Development Finance & Aid, TD/7, p. 17.

TABLE 21

Annual Net Inflow Corresponding to a Given Gross Inflow of
Financial Resources, 1966-75

	Africa			Asia, Middle East			Latin America			Total[a]		
	1966	1970	1975	1966	1970	1975	1966	1970	1975	1966	1970	1975
Gross Inflow	2.9	2.9	2.9	4.6	4.6	4.6	2.6	2.6	2.6	11.0	11.0	11.0
Total Debt Service[b]	0.8	1.6	1.8	1.4	2.2	2.4	2.3	2.3	2.4	5.1	7.0	7.5
Net Inflow[c]	2.1	1.3	1.1	3.2	2.4	2.2	0.4	0.3	0.2	5.9	4.0	3.6
Net Lending[d]	0.7	-0.1	-0.2	1.1	0.2	0.1	-0.2	-0.3	-0.4	1.8	-0.1	-0.5
Debt Outstanding	5.8	8.5	9.7	12.2	17.0	21.2	10.2	11.8	13.5	31.5	41.8	49.9

[a] Includes projection for southern Europe.
[b] Includes estimates of debt service on old debt as well as new gross lending.
[c] Grants and grantlike contributions plus net lending.
[d] Net of interest and amortization.

Source: UNCTAD, The Outlook for Debt Service, TD/7/Supp 5.

proposal is an attempt to contribute to the solution of both problems simultaneously.

Repayments of principal and interest on previous loans should be credited to a separate aid budget, instead of returning to the Exchequer. In this way, the budgetary requirements for new aid appropriations would be reduced. If donors are not willing to contribute aid, it would be open to them to reduce new appropriations to the same extent as the separate aid budget grows. But if they are serious in saying that it is a budgetary, not a real resource, constraint which prevents them from doing more, such an arrangement would make it possible to give a greater volume of aid without additional budgetary appropriations.

NOTES

1. UNCTAD, External Development Finance: Present and Future, TD/E/C.3/61.

2. Ibid., TD/D/C.3/61.

3. President of the World Bank, address to the Board of Governors of the World Bank group and the IMF (September 27, 1965).

4. UNCTAD, The Terms, Quality and Effectiveness of Financial Flows and Problems of Debt Service, TD/B/C.3/35.

5. UNCTAD, Terms of Financial Flows and the Problems of Debt Service, TD/7/Supp. 3.

6. Ibid.

7. UNCTAD, The Outlook for Debt Service, TD/7/ Supp. 5. On p. 11, merchandise exports are estimated as $40.6 billion in 1966. Assuming a growth rate of exports of 4 percent, the 1965 figure was derived.

8. Ibid.

9. The World Bank estimates for debt servicing

as a percentage of Africa Class II.   UNCTAD, Handbook
of International Trade and Development Statistics
1969. Since the World Bank data do not include all
the African Class II countries, the debt servicing
ratio is not exact measurement but a close approxi-
mation.

     10.   The Outlook for Debt Service, TD/7/Supp.
5; The Terms of Financial Flows and Problems of Debt
Servicing, TD/7/Supp. 3; The Terms of Financial Flows,
TD/B/C.3/55; The Terms, Quality and Effectiveness of
Financial Flows and Problems of Debt Service, TD/B/C.
3/35.

Some writers would base the case for aid on a
simple, logical extension of the principles of the
welfare state to a welfare world, a straight application of the notion of human brotherhood. Just as we
accept that a national community has responsibilities
toward each citizen and that it must provide him with
minimum standards of social security, so our ethical
code should apply to each member of the world community. International solidarity has not yet reached
the point at which such an argument is generally
accepted--or, if accepted, implementable. Indeed,
the movement toward greater national solidarity and
stronger national welfare states has weakened the
international links of solidarity that had existed
in the past. National consolidation has led to international disharmony.

But the present case for giving aid does not
rest on the acceptance of an international welfare
state. It is simply this: rich countries are partly
(though only partly) responsible for the poverty in
less developed countries, and they can do something
about it. The combination of (partial) responsibility
for and (partial) ability to help remove poverty con-
stitutes the hard core of the present case for aid.
It probably will not convert those not already con-
verted, but that does not detract from its strength.
Even if there were no responsibility, the needs of
other human beings starving, ill nourished or

ill-housed, diseased, and illiterate impose an obligation to help--just as we would use our hose to put
out a fire in our neighbor's house.

The ability to help can hardly be doubted. The
responsibility for some of the difficulties faced by
developing countries does not rest primarily, as is
sometimes asserted, on colonial exploitation (though
neglect has been more important), but on the obstacles
created for developing countries by the existence and
the policies of advanced, industrial nation-states,
a set of obstacles which the now advanced countries
did not have to overcome, or had to overcome only to
a much smaller degree, in their preindustrial phase.

Since the coexistence of a number of different
societies, each at a different stage of development,
crucially determines the development prospects of
the least-developed ones, a consideration of differentials must form part of any valid analysis, prog-
nosis, and cure. The fact that advanced industrial
societies already exist and are organized in strong
nation-states when other countries embark on development makes a number of important differences to the
development prospects and the development strategies
of underdeveloped societies. Africa has been the
latest starter in economic development, compared not
only with the now advanced, industrial countries but
also with the rest of the developing world, within
which inequality is rapidly increasing.

Some of these differences, and perhaps the most
obvious ones, clearly benefit underdeveloped countries.
A growing stock of scientific, technical, and organizational knowledge has been accumulated, on which
the underdeveloped countries can draw. They do not
have to go through the laborious process of acquiring
this knowledge for themselves and can therefore avoid
a number of errors and false starts. The high level
of income in advanced industrial countries and its
steady and continuing growth create a demand for the
products of the underdeveloped countries and enable
them to benefit from wider international specialization
than was possible for the pioneers. Private investment, financial aid, and technical assistance contribute to the transfer of resources and skills from

the rich countries to the poor and thus enable the latter to draw on a bigger pool of resources. These benefits were not available, or available only to a smaller extent, when the now industrialized countries embarked on their development.

Some authors derive much hope from the economic forces that tend to diffuse technical progress from the advanced countries to the poor. If only the level of demand and employment is kept high and growing, so that the rich economies are forced to search outside their own boundaries for low-cost sources of raw materials and minerals and for manufactured products requiring much labor; if restrictions on the movement of goods, capital, and men are removed; and if technical assistance and aid are provided on an adequate scale, the progress achieved in the center, according to this view, will automatically spread to the periphery and the benefits will be widely distributed.[1]

On the other hand, the coexistence of rich and poor countries and the policies pursued by rich countries have a number of drawbacks for the underdeveloped countries, which affect them more adversely, the later they start. Some of these result from the relationships between countries at different stages of development, others from the fact that rich countries exist. Africa has suffered from both types of drawback.

The most important political difference lies in the consolidation of the nation-state. Advance has meant national progress and national consolidation in the industrial countries. The benefits of the welfare state are confined largely to its citizens. National consolidation in rich countries has encouraged nationalism in underdeveloped countries, and the attempts of the rich to integrate the nation by protectionist and welfare policies have tended to lead to international disintegration.[2] Attempts to maintain full employment and to insulate the national economy from outside influences have strengthened the forces of nationalist protection in the welfare state and reduced the opportunities for trade, capital flows, and migration. Export of capital and scarce

skills, and immigration that threatens to upset industrial peace or national prejudices, are restricted by
the rich countries, which thereby prevent the people
in the poor countries from participating in their
fortune.

In the early enthusiasm with full employment and
welfare policies after the last war, it was thought
that the achievement and maintenance of full employment
would reduce the need for protectionist policies and
would restore the era of free international trade, free
movement of man, and international solidarity. In the
event, full employment has created its own strong
motivation for restrictions on trade, payments, and
immigration. First, full employment tended to cause
inflationary pressures and balance of payments difficulties to those who inflated faster than others.
These led to restrictions. Second, full employment
tended to be interpreted as applying to particular
regions and occupations, and the structural unemployment which some low-cost imports from developing countries would have entailed was considered intolerable.
Third, full employment brought with it the desire to
make the fullest use of national resources. This
brought the terms-of-trade argument for tariffs to the
fore, which had no force in a situation of unemployment.
In particular, it became important to keep the prices
of imported food and raw materials low, or at any rate
to resist measures that might raise them. Fourth, the
desire to maintain and raise wages constituted a powerful argument against immigration of workers who would
weaken the bargaining power of trade unions. Fifth,
the need to mobilize savings for domestic growth and
welfare objectives set a limit to the outflow of aid
and private capital. For these and similar reasons,
the national welfare state has turned out to be a
not very good neighbor to other countries which
depended on trade, migration, and capital. The protectionist nationalism of the depression years has
been replaced by the welfare nationalism of affluence.

It is significant, for example, how little provision for extra aid there was in the first National
Plan of the Labour government in Britain. No plea
of balance of payments problems can be entered for

this somewhat nationalistic program for greater
domestic affluence with little regard for the crying
needs of the world beyond the national boundaries.
Similarly, the growing concern for the environment
and for measures against pollution and domestic poverty have turned the Nixon administration away from
its international obligations.

The moral argument for aid derives partly from
the fact that it is our organization of society
which enables the rich to remain rich and the poor
to be kept poor. A complete (though Utopian) acceptance of the liberal values underlying the Judeo-
Christian and humanist civilization would imply worldwide equality of opportunity and therefore perhaps
free trade and free movement of men. Instead, we
witness an extremely uneven worldwide distribution
between ratios of men to resources, according to
national boundaries, and the use of the power of the
state to confine the wealth to the wealthy and to
prevent the poor from sharing it. This is not a plea
for the implementation of a world order based on the
brotherhood of man. It is an argument for mitigating
the harm done by the division of the world into rich
and poor nations, a division which is essentially
arbitrary from any ethical point of view.

In quite a different sphere, the most important
difference is that the advanced state of medical
knowledge makes it now possible to reduce deaths
cheaply and rapidly, without having, at least until
recently, contributed to an equally cheap and readily
acceptable reduction in births. This has upset the
population equilibrium and has caused the large and
accelerating rates of population growth which present
the underdeveloped countries with much more difficult
obstacles than those which the now advanced countries
faced in their preindustrial phase, when the rate of
population growth was considerably less, was partly
the result of successful development and rising
levels of living, and when large-scale emigration
was still possible.

It is often argued that rapid and accelerating
population growth does not present a problem to

Africa, with its vast reserves of land and natural
resources and its low density of population. But
the problems posed by population growth are not
problems of land or food or density. They spring
from the need to divert scarce resources from the
provision of productive equipment to the provision
of houses, schools, and other overhead facilities;
they relate to the changing age structure of the
population, to the growing proportion of nonproductive
young (42 percent of all Africans are less than fifteen years old), and, above all, to growing unemployment and underemployment. Additions to the labor
force do not, under present conditions, contribute
to production. These difficulties are just as serious
in Africa as in Asia, and the need for limiting population growth is no less urgent.

Although a stock of scientific and technical
knowledge is available on which African countries
can draw, the modern technology is ill-adapted to
the conditions and the factor endowments of these
countries. Modern technology was evolved in conditions of labor scarcity, and its purpose is therefore
to save labor in relation to capital. The transfer
of these sometimes inappropriate methods, which is
encouraged by attitudes toward modernization and by
the prestige of Western technology, tends to aggravate
the gross underutilization of labor from which African
countries are suffering. When inappropriate technology
is transferred and when the labor force grows rapidly,
obstacles are created which are fundamentally different
from those which the now industrial societies had to
overcome in their preindustrial phase.

Not only most available techniques of production
but also existing models of organizations and institutions are ill-adapted to the needs of the underdeveloped world. Modern trade union structure and attitudes, like technology, have evolved in different
social conditions and can therefore be damaging if
transferred to conditions in which labor is not fully
utilized. The demand for the adoption of social welfare services which have no or negative impact on
development and which were introduced in advanced
industrial welfare states at a late stage has often
proved an impediment to development and, far from

contributing to greater social justice, has strengthened vested interests and pockets of privilege. Large
public expenditure on curative medicine, on higher
education, and on subsides to indiscriminate consumption has absorbed scarce resources and reinforced
attitudes and practices hostile to development.

Even political institutions, such as parliamentary
democracy and the Westminster model, are not always
adapted to the needs of developing countries and,
under the guise of constitutional democracy, reinforce
the reluctance to touch vested interests and to pursue
development by tough and hard measures.

For a number of reasons, capital and skilled
men, including those of the underdeveloped countries,
are attracted to the richest industrial societies.
Capital flight is substantial, attracted by higher
rates of return and greater political security.
Skilled men and professionals, on whose education and
training large public funds have been spent, have
greater opportunities for emigration, are better and
more rapidly informed about them, and have stronger
incentives to seize them. As a result, some of the
scarcest, most valuable, and most expensive factors
of production are drained away from the poor periphery
to the rich center.

So far, Africa has not suffered from the brain
drain as much as other regions. But this is a symptom
of its relatively low stage of development. As soon
as the number of educated and professional men increases, the temptations of international salary
scales will either lure them away or will distort
the domestic income distribution in attempts to produce counterlures--or, most probably, both.

But the mobility of factors is partial and
biased. Whereas in the preindustrial phase of now
industrialized societies (with the exception of Japan)
areas rich in natural resources were still unsettled
and were able to receive immigrants, the world has
now been parceled up and immigration of unskilled
men and women, particularly if they are colored, is
severely restricted. This, together with population
growth, growing underutilization of labor, and the

loss of the scarcest and most expensive resources
greatly increases the obstacles to development.

High levels of remuneration for professional
skills in advanced countries raise obstacles to development in underdeveloped countries which go beyond
the direct losses through emigration. By the creation
of an international market in these skills, not only
are internal inequalities without functional justification increased in underdeveloped countries, but obstacles are put into the path of development. International inequality has an impact on internal income
distribution in underdeveloped countries which, like
the impact of modern technology and modern institutions, impedes development.

Systematic scientific research and institutionally
built-in innovation, which are reflected in the annual
growth of productivity characteristic of growing economies, has only been heavily biased toward activities
which are not suited for production in underdeveloped
countries, and it has in some cases actually led to a
reduction in the demand for the traditional primary
exports of African countries. Technical progress has
reduced the need for the imports of the staple products of developing countries (a) because synthetics
have been substituted for natural products, (b) because
there has been increasing economy in the use of raw
materials, and (c) because demand has shifted toward
services and products with low primary import content.

To these reasons must be added the protectionist
policies pursued by the developed countries in agriculture and through cascading tariffs, which rise with
the stage of processing and penalize attempts to industrialize. The trade opportunities of underdeveloped
countries have been reduced and their ability to diver-
sify and industrialize has been hampered, though their
incentive to do so has been increased. These obstacles
go beyond the often bewailed, but not fully confirmed,
unfavorable trend in the commodity terms of trade.

They are systematically related to the speed
of scientific and technical progress in the advanced
industrial countries. One of the serious costs of

progress, which we all too readily accept as not only
sacrosanct but also inevitable, is the rapidity and
frequency with which the skills, processes, and products of the poorest members of the international
community are permitted to become obsolete. The
gains of those enjoying the fruits of progress and
the losses of those suffering the damage of obsoles-
cence are distributed in a highly biased way; it is
those who have, who gain, and those who have not,
who lose. The stories of sisal, rubber, and the
possibility of synthetic cocoa, coffee, and tea are
illustrations which show how parts of Africa have
been particularly hard hit by rapid industrial progress in the rich north. They are themselves the
expression of a desire to insulate rich and comfort-
able societies against the disturbances of change,
even at the cost of some reduction in the benefits
derived from international specialization. Recent
technical progress in methods of birth control, of
producing staple food crops and cheap protein, of
transport, desalination, and even, on a small scale,
of more appropriate industrial technology have begun
to compensate for the earlier biased research; but
it is as yet early to say how effective these com-
pensations will prove. Research and development
expenditure on the solution of the problems of the
poor is still infinitesimal.

While it is true that foreign private enterprise
can help to transfer material resources and human
skills and know-how from rich to poor countries, it
also creates greater difficulties than those which
were presented by borrowing from abroad to industrialized societies in their preindustrial phase. Then
money was borrowed at fixed interest rates of between
5 and 6 percent, and default was not uncommon. Now
almost all long-term private capital takes the form
of direct equity at 15 percent to 25 percent pre-local
tax, and 10 percent to 15 percent post-local tax;
and default on loans, whether private or official,
is hardly ever allowed to occur.[3] Remitting profits,
interest, and dividends creates or aggrevates the
balance of payments problems of African countries,
partly because of their height and partly because of
inadequate reinvestment.

We have suggested that technical and organizational knowledge are ill-adapted and that their
transfer can be harmful to the African countries.
In addition, Western economic concepts and theories,
and policies based on these, are often inappropriate
and misleading when applied to current development
problems. Economic analysis and policy have tended
to focus on investment (whether in fixed capital
assets or in an aggregate called "education"), to
the neglect of essential reforms of human attitudes
and social institutions; and they have tended to
formulate categories of aggregates which obscure the
relevant distinctions and neglect the actual behavior
on which the concepts, models, and policies are based.[4]

Some people have argued that even the form which
some government aid has taken has obstructed progress
toward development, by supporting and upholding
feudal or conservative or corrupt regimes which are
unwilling to carry out the social and political reforms
necessary for progress, or by reinforcing the dual
and uneven structure in many countries. Aid policies
directed at investments and neglecting social reforms
(of land tenure, taxation, or education) are encouraged, intellectually, by the escape mechanism provided
by Western economic theorizing and politically by
powerful vested interests on both the donors' and
the recipients' sides. The experience with the Alliance for Progress in Latin America is not encouraging
to the possibilities of combining aid with the implementation of radical social reforms.

Although for these reasons the opportunities to
develop have been reduced, the sense of urgency among
the still small middle classes and the ruling elites
has greatly increased. Seeing opulence and rapid
growth abroad means feeling the pain of their absence
all the more acutely at home. It is true not only
that what you don't know doesn't hurt you, which must
have made things easier for the now industrialized
societies in their preindustrial stage, but also that
what you do know does hurt. This clearly reduces the
patience with which the development process is viewed
by the ruling elites in the underdeveloped world.

It is this coexistence of rich and poor nation-
states, rather than the intentional or unintentional
colonial or neocolonial exploitation (though colonial
neglect also played a part), which can have detrimental
effects on the development efforts in Africa. And it
is this coexistence which sets limits to the ready
transfer of the lessons of one historical setting to
an entirely different one. No analysis can be valid
which does not allow for this change in the world
setting in which development occurs.

The considerations also bear on the frequently
deplored widening gap between the living standards
of the rich and poor countries. On the face of it,
it might seem that much more important than the gap
is the rate at which the lot of the mass of the people
in the poor countries is improving. Should we not
all prefer a growth rate of 6 percent per year in
the poor countries, combined with one of 8 percent
in the rich, to one of 3 percent in the poor combined
with 2 percent in the rich, even though the former
combination would widen, while the latter would narrow,
the gap? Maybe so. But the rate of progress in the
rich countries affects the development prospects and
strategies of the poor; and it is not obvious that,
on balance, faster growth of the rich world is always
beneficial to or neutral for the poor. Many of the
difficulties raised for developing countries are
aggravated if international income differentials
increase; and it may therefore be sensible, and not
just the result of a philosophy of envy, to aim at
reducing growing income differentials, even if this
means some slowing down of average world income growth.
In particular, we have seen how rapid progress can
damage the development prospects of those whose exports
it renders obsolete, those on whose trained and skilled
manpower the fast-growing countries draw, and those
who find that less capital is left over for them when
the capital hunger of rapid growth must be satisfied.

Finally, it follows that development strategies
must differ not only, as is now generally recognized,
in space, from country to country and region to
region, but also in time, from stage to stage, each

stage related to the stages reached by other countries.
The need to take full account, not only of the position in space but also of the relative position in
time, in forging a development strategy greatly com-
plicates the process of planning and reduces the value
of lessons from the past and of universal prescrip-
tions. A country, particularly if it is small, must
pay attention not only to its own peculiar history,
resource endowment, and institutions but also to the
events and activities in the countries ahead of it
and must weigh the benefits and drawbacks of outward-
looking strategies against those of shielding its
frontiers and insulating itself against the impulses
from the outside.

Africa is doubly handicapped in this spatial
and temporal perspective. Lying for a large part
under the tropical sun--where practically all underdeveloped regions are to be found--and being the
latest starter on the climb to development, she suffers the combined drawbacks of climate, of being for
a large part landlocked, and of being the latest
comer on the development scene.

The conclusion of this brief survey is that the
rich, as members both of nation-states and of an
interdependent world community, cannot escape accept-
ing responsibility for aiding the poor, and that
attempts to contract out of this responsibility are
morally and politically impermissible. It also con-
stitutes an argument for a special responsibility
toward the least developed countries, the majority
of which are in Africa, for these are worst hit by
many of the factors discussed above. (See Chapter 14.)
They were particularly open, and therefore vulnerable,
to the impact of the rich, industrial countries because
of their colonial status. There exists, therefore,
a special responsibility, as well as a special opportunity, to compensate for the harmful consequences
of the coexistence of rich and poor states and for
some of the policies that would otherwise condemn
the poor to remain poor.

NOTES

1.   The existence of a powerful economic mechanism of diffusion, frustrated by wrong-headed policies, has been strongly argued by Harry G. Johnson, Economic Policies Towards Less Developed Countries (Washington and London: The Brookings Institute, 1967), Esp. pp. 48-52. See also Donald Kessing, "Outward-Looking Policies and Economic Development," Economic Journal LXXVII, 306, pp. 303-320 (June, 1967). But some of the differences between Professor Johnson's arguments and those put forward in this chapter depend upon what one considers established and what removable features of the current scene, and also on what one deems to be economic and what political forces.

2.   Gunnar Myrdal, An International Economy (London: Routledge and Kegan Paul, 1956) Chapters III and IV.

3.   For a discussion of the virtues and defects on private overseas investment, see Paul Streeten, "New Approaches to Private Investment" in Private Foreign Investment and the Developing World, edited by Peter Ady (New York: Praeger Publishers, 1971).

4.   Paul Streeten, "The Use and Abuse of Models in Development Planning," in Kurt Martin and John Knapp, eds., The Teaching of Development Economics (London: Frank Cass, 1967).

**RELATIONS BETWEEN
POOR AND POOR,
AND THE NEED
FOR REGIONAL
COOPERATION**

Although we often speak of the Third World as
if it were a homogeneous group and of the interests
of each of its members as if they were in harmony
with those of the others, the coexistence of very
poor and not quite so poor countries also creates
special problems for development. Once again, they
both impair and improve one another's prospects. On
the one hand, it is possible for those more successful than others to render technical assistance which
is more relevant than that of countries far removed
from these problems. India is in a good position to
advise on family planning, popular education, and
land consolidation; Israel (at least until recently
an underdeveloped country) can teach how to integrate
immigrants of traditional background from Africa and
Asia into modern agriculture; Iran has valuable
experience in popular education. If developed countries reduce their demand for imports because of
technical progress or protectionist policies, underdeveloped countries can get together and create
demand for one another's products while exploiting
the economies of scale of larger markets. Regional
integration makes it possible to combine the advantages of protection for infant industries with those
of a wider division of labor. Industrial plants can
be erected which, though not fully competitive inter-
nationally, can exploit a degree of specialization
among themselves. Developing countries have the

land, the raw materials, the fuel, and the ability
to acquire the skills and raise the savings and
finance to dispense very largely with dependence on
the industrial countries.

Against these advantages must be set the dangers
of competing against each other for the limited
market and capital of the rich. Beggar-my-neighbor
tax holidays and other tax concessions to foreign
capital reduce its benefits without succeeding in
attracting much more. While the prices of manufactured
products and some minerals are held up by concerted
action of their already rich producers, the prices
of many African primary agricultural products are
victims of fierce competition. Benefits from any
rise in productivity and production tend to be passed
on in lower prices to rich buyers. In addition, there
is political rivalry. Hostility forces countries to
devote scarce resources to expenditure on armaments.
Nationalism creates obstacles to devising methods by
which poor countries at different stages of development can cooperate with one another. The least
developed tend to be afraid lest integration will
hurt their prospects of industrialization and will
drain away their few valuable resources, while the
less underdeveloped fear lest their tax revenue or
skills will be used to subsidize the most backward
areas. Prohibitions imposed by one underdeveloped
country on the movement of men, money, goods, and
services of others, in the name of national consolidation and integration, reduce the benefits to be derived
from the international division of labor or even from
regional communities and have inflicted harm on other
underdeveloped countries.

It is therefore a mistake to lump the whole of
Africa together in discussing aid policies. A non-
discriminating approach can aggravate differentials
within the developing world, just as a laissez-faire
approach improves the chances of the strong at the
expense of the weak.

The above considerations raise the problems of
regional and subregional cooperation and integration.
Among the obstacles of fuller cooperation lie the

differentials in income and wealth between potential
members of a community and the need to compensate
those who suffer from such cooperation.

A primary objective of aid to Africa must be to
encourage the formation of wider markets, a rational
investment policy based on subregional, regional,
and intercontinental cooperation and greater mobility
of skills and private investment. Economic integration can achieve these ends and contribute to overcoming the obstacles created by the fragmentation of
the numerous and often economically irrational post-
colonial states. National boundaries created at
independence cut across ethnic, topographic, linguistic, and economic lines. The division of human and
physical resources bears no relation to the needs of
growth and development.

The two chief problems here are (1) how to adjust
a network of communications, transport, banking, and
trade, based on exports to Europe, to one of growing
intraregional trade and (2) how to ensure that the
least developed member countries of a region attract
their share of industries, services, and revenues
and receive adequate compensation for having to buy
higher-cost industrial imports from the more highly
industrialized members of a union than they would be
able to buy from outside the union.

Aid can contribute to the removal of both these
obstacles to integration. It can be used to develop
lines of communication and transport now exceedingly
rudimentary, which would encourage the flow of interregional trade, and to compensate least developed
countries for the damage suffered by joining with
more industrialized neighbors.

Technical assistance in particular can contribute
to facilitating the institutional arrangements required for regional cooperation.

In addition, however, it may be necessary to
modify some of the rules in the code of international
trade and payments to adapt them to the needs of
regional cooperation between developing countries at
different stages of development.

This is not the place to discuss these issues
in great detail, except to the extent to which they
affect the quantity and quality of aid. Limited
untying which permits tied loans to be spent either
in the donor country or in a member country of the
region or subregion, would help. (See Chapter 13.)
The use of aid to encourage joint indicative planning
is another possibility. Development plans are still
too often purely national, without much regard to
the plans of neighboring countries. Indicative
planning would help to avoid self-defeating agricultural diversification in ecologically and climatically
similar regions and would assist the exploitation of
economies of scale in manufacturing industry and
economies in transport costs.

Another method of assisting regional cooperation
in trade is to provide funds to support the creation
of regional payments unions. Such unions are designed
to facilitate trade liberalization between developing
countries while reducing the fears that such liberalization may aggravate balance of payments difficulties
and loss of reserves. Members of the union grant one
another credits. Outside funds are used to contribute
to the sources of financing such credits.

In many instances, though not always, a flourish-
ing export trade has been built upon a large and
assured home market. The reasons for this are partly
lower risks and partly economies of scale. It would
follow that the creation of successful export industries often presupposes the creation of an industrial
complex larger than a minimum critical size. It provides an argument for concentration, to reap to the
fullest the benefits of complementarities, scale
economies, and specialization. This is particularly
important in many African countries, where industrialization is hampered by absence or limitation of
markets.

Against this principle there runs another: the
principle of spreading industries in order to diffuse
benefits and share them as widely as possible. It
may be thought desirable to sacrifice efficiency,
and hence growth, for the sake of greater equality,

or for the sake of greater political consensus, or
for fair shares between regions, which often coincide
with tribal areas. But the two objectives can be
combined through an efficient fiscal system which
collects revenue in the industrial centers and dis-
burses revenue for social services, training and
education, and transport for the benefit of the periphery.

A particularly valuable function of aid consists
in strengthening the fiscal efforts of a country or
a subregion to enable it to combine efficiency, growth,
equity, and political integration in this manner and
to prevent, on the one hand, polarization of benefits
and, on the other hand, inefficient location of industries.

Within a country this can be achieved by backing
a development plan which pays heed to the efficient
location of industry. Between states the problem is
more difficult because political obstacles have to
be overcome and national development plans have to
be coordinated. Yet the effectiveness of a given
quantum of aid can be increased by backing the most
efficient development and compensating, where necessary
or desirable, those interests which are liable to lose
from it. Such processes could be interpreted as
paternalistic and neocolonial, but those interested
in effective development in the African countries
are likely to welcome them.

In efforts to integrate the numerous small economies of Africa, the proposed African Development
Fund and the ECA would make valuable contributions.

The discussion of the impact of international
transfers of resources on development suffers from
what might be described as an intellectual time lag.
We use frequently concepts, categories, and models
derived from experiences before the last war or even
before 1913, and apply them directly to our own world
today. This is not the place to analyze the nine-
teenth-century experience of resource transfers to
developing countries, but suffice it to say that
there was then a strong tendency for long-term capital
movements to correct payments imbalances. It is
precisely this mechanism (rather than the movement
of labor) which maintains balance between regions
within a country, where exchange rate adjustments are
ruled out.

The English-speaking world and the Atlantic
community formed then a fairly unified region within
which capital moved freely and restrictions on the
movement of labor were much smaller. Fixed exchange
rates were widespread, though not universal. Surpluses and deficits between the periphery and the
center were accommodated by balancing capital movements. New borrowing in the form of capital issues
quickly led to transfer of real resources to finance
deficits of borrowers, and the deficits of borrowers
quickly led to balancing capital issues and long-term
loans. Both deficits and loans reflected increased
investment opportunities in the periphery. The large

and free capital market in London, in which money
could be borrowed at rates only slightly above those
prevailing on domestic securities, enabled equilibrium
to be restored painlessly and quickly.

It would be an understatement to say that the
situation with respect to the international transfer
of resources today is different from that in the
nineteenth century. While the required adjustments
were then smaller, the need to make them and the
scope for making them were much larger. There are
a number of features which distinguish modern international capital flows and the modern adjustment
mechanism from those in the last century.*

First, countries no longer use the automatic
adjustment mechanisms of the balance of payments
which existed in the nineteenth century. They are
now able and determined to maintain high levels of
employment, so that variations in employment cannot
take the brunt of adjustments. Price deflation in
advanced manufacturing countries is now ruled out.
Exchange rates are kept fixed for long periods, without adherence to the principles of the gold standard.
For these reasons, a greatly increased weight would
have to be borne by capital movements as almost the
only remaining equilibrating force. As far as short-
term capital movements are concerned, they could, in
principle, play an equilibrating part, were it not
for disequilibrating speculation. But they would
not be a substitute for adjustments. Some writers
see in long-term capital movements a possible equilibrating mechanism. No doubt, in certain situations
they can fulfill this function. The structural balance
of payments disequilibria of some developing countries
can be eased by capital inflow on appropriate terms.

----

*See P. N. Rosenstein-Rodan, Philosophy of
Foreign Investment in the Second Half of the Twentieth
Century Ch. 4; and George Borts, in J. M. Adler, ed.,
Capital Movements and Economic Development (New York:
St. Martin's Press, 1967), p. 65.

Europe's postwar balance of payments disequilibrium
was remedied by American capital inflow, although
the terms of America's capital to Europe under the
Marshall Plan were, it can be judged in the light of
hindsight, excessively soft--more than 90 percent in
the form of grants--and today's aid to African countries has been too hard; in 1966 only 60 percent of
total commitments took the form of grants. But there
are other forms of disequilibria to whose cure long-
term capital flows make no contribution; they may
even be aggravated by them because fundamental adjustments are postponed.

     Second, the world economy, in spite of the re-
markable buoyancy of total world trade and the high
correlation between export growth rates and income
growth rates, is no longer the same kind of "engine
of growth" which it was in the last century. Britain,
which had a high propensity to import primary products
without restrictions, and which provided the capital
and the men for the expansion of the production of
primary commodities abroad, has been replaced as a
center by the United States with a considerably lower
import propensity. The United States is a much more
self-sufficient economy; generates technical progress
which is biased against imports; heavily protects its
domestic market, particularly of labor-intensive and
processed products; and absorbs a much higher proportion of its savings at home. Europe, though more
dependent on trade, is even more protectionist.
Political uncertainties have further reduced the
flow of international investment. As a result, the
transfer problem created by servicing debt and investment is much more serious than it was in the last
century.

     Africa is heavily dependent on the exports of
primary commodities, producing 82 percent of the
non-Communist world's cobalt, 72 percent of its cocoa,
62 percent of its chromite, 49 percent of its manga-
nese, 36 percent of its groundnuts, and nearly 30
percent of its phosphate rock, copper, and coffee.
Some 80 percent of its exports are primary commodities
and, if very slightly processed minerals are added,

the proportion rises to almost 95 percent.* Although
growth rates of African exports have risen from 4.9
percent in 1948-59 to 5.4 percent in 1960-68, the
threat of synthetic substitutes and of fluctuations
in world demand arising from other causes is ever
present. Apart from the oil and copper exporters,
the foreign exchange constraint is likely to become
increasingly severe as countries step up their development expenditure.

Third, the international monetary system, from
having been the oil which lubricated the "engine of
growth" by facilitating trading and lending, has
become grit in the engine and a major obstacle to
the expansion of international trade and investment.
Recent reforms have alleviated the situation, but we
are still far from an international monetary system
which facilitates growth, trade, and the fullest use
of the world's resources.

Fourth, much international lending is no longer
guided by profitability. Intergovernmental lending
in the form of aid now occupies an important place.
Whatever the merits and defects of international aid,
there is little to be learned from the nineteenth-
century pattern, except that successful development
often requires soft loans, whether ex ante, as today,
or ex post (as a result of depressions and wars), as
in the nineteenth century.

---

*Lester B. Pearson et al., Partners in Develop-
ment, pp. 267-68.

10

CAPITAL REQUIREMENTS, GAP ANALYSIS, AND ABSORPTIVE CAPACITY

The conventional approach to the aid requirements of developing countries attempts to calculate
a gap, either between required investment and domestic
savings or between required foreign exchange and
earnings from exports. In the calculation of the
investment-savings gap, also called the resource gap,
the required investment is normally derived from a
target rate of growth of national income and a constant or systematically varying capital/output ratio.
Given a target rate of growth and a capital/output
ratio, the investment/income ratio can be derived.
Domestic private and public savings are then deducted
from the required investment and the difference
emerges as the resource gap, to be filled by foreign
capital. Similarly, in calculating the foreign exchange (or the trade) gap, import requirements are
geared to growth of national income, likely export
receipts are deducted, and the difference appears
as the foreign exchange gap. Both models are based
on a Harrod-Domar model with structural constraints
added in the model of the foreign exchange gap. The
limit on growth is set by whichever gap is larger.
Ex ante, the resource gap is said to precede, histori-
cally, the trade gap as the "dominant gap" in a
country's development. The gap between the gaps can
be inferred only from projected requirements. Ex
post, it always disappears and the two gaps are
identical, since the accounting identity "excess of
imports over exports = excess of domestic investment
over domestic savings" must hold.

This highly aggregated analysis can be disaggre-
gated. The model can specify a set of consistent
relations between production, consumption, and trade
for any number of commodities and services into
which the national product is divided. Such an inter-
sectoral analysis of the structure of production,
consumption, and trade can be used to determine the
level of gross national product, gross investment,
exports and imports, and aid corresponding to each
solution. But this model is static and refers only
to one point in time, usually the last year of the
plan. It also omits effects of price changes.

The dynamic model, which analyzes growth patterns
and gaps over time, relates growth of GNP to savings,
investment, imports, and exports. It can be made
more flexible by the introduction of assumptions
about (a) the cost of aid relative to the value of
increased consumption and (b) absorptive capacity
and other limitations on the economy's ability to
invest and shift resources into import substitution.

The investment-savings gap or the resource gap
has the following weaknesses:

1. The growth rate of national income does not
depend primarily on the investment/income ratio, i.e.,
on the extent to which the people are prepared to
sacrifice present consumption in favor of greater
future consumption. Growth depends as much on factors
other than capital in the narrow sense, particularly
administrative, technical, and managerial skills.
At times this point is made in an extreme manner by
postulating limited "absorptive capacity," but the
general point is simply the law of diminishing returns in a growth setting.

2. The capital/output ratio cannot be assumed
to be constant or a stable function of income, or
of the rate of growth of income. It depends on a
large number of variables, including climate, human
attitudes, and social institutions, as well as conventional economic variables such as the degree of
capacity utilization and the construction period.
In particular, it depends on the policies pursued by
the government.

3.   The distinction between consumption and investment is false. Much development expenditure is directed at health, education, and even feeding. Certain types of consumption in many less developed countries have a positive marginal productivity. On the other hand, much investment makes no contribution to development or is wasted (unused irrigation, underutilized industrial capacity, some luxury housing).

4.   The attempt to calculate a single gap is preeconomic. Even on the assumptions of the model, domestic growth rates cannot be expressed in a single figure but are the function of domestic savings and other variables. Domestic savings will also depend on the trade-aid mix. In addition, both types of gap calculations use quite unreliable data to arrive at misleading aggregates. Projection of past trends neglects policy changes, while the attempt to incorporate such changes endows personal judgment with an air of mathematical certainty and feeds false confidence.

Men of good will face a dilemma in the present African aid crisis. On the one hand, it is evident that there is no correlation between the amount of aid per head received and economic growth of the recipient. All sorts of reasons or excuses can be advanced to explain away this (to the aid lobby) unpalatable fact, but it remains an awkward fact.* On the other hand, it is surely a basic creed, not only of economics but also of common sense, that if aid, defined as the provision of additional resources, is used effectively, it must make it possible to produce more than would have been possible without it. And if economic growth is desired, greater production can be allocated to yield more growth.

----

*Some explanations are given in Lester B. Pearson et al., Partners in Development, p. 49. One might add to these that food aid should be deducted before correlations aid and growth.

The conflict between the (nonconclusive) evidence
of absence of a relationship between aid and development (as measured by growth rates) and the logical
force of the proposition that more means more, can
be used as a challenge to developers to ensure the
effective use of aid.

In the conventional gap analysis, domestic saving
is added to foreign saving to give the total resources
available for investment, which, in turn, determine
the addition to national income and therefore the
growth rate. In Figure 1 the line GG_1 shows alternative combinations of foreign and domestic savings
rates required for a growth rate of, say, 6 percent,
on the assumption that they are, dollar for dollar,
perfectly substitutable. The line will have a slope
of -1, cutting the two axes at angles of 45°. If
foreign funds show a tendency to flow into projects
with higher capital/output ratios than domestic
funds, the line will be flatter, like GG_2. If, on
the other hand, recipients are fonder of capital-intensive projects than are donors (like moving capital
cities or constructing large steel plants), the line
will be steeper. If we start from a point E, a crude
gap analyst might say that foreign savings must rise
by FF_1 in order to achieve 6 percent growth, i.e.,
the vertical line EF, showing the amount of aid
supplied, must shift to the right to point F_1. But
domestic savings are not independent of foreign
savings, though the precise nature of the dependence
is not altogether clear. The relationship may be as
pictured in the three S_D functions:* the domestic

---

*Alternatively, the absolute amount of savings
could be traced on the two axes. It is the savings
rate which is relevant to the growth rate; but it
must be remembered that income and savings can go up
as a result of an inflow of foreign aid while the
savings rate remains the same or even declines.
Whether we trace savings or a fortiori the savings
rate, aid can contribute to an increase in consumption.
If the terms of aid are sufficiently soft, this must
be reckoned a benefit even if neither the savings
rate nor savings is increased.

savings rate might rise with a higher foreign savings
rate if the country generates higher savings rates
out of the higher incomes made possible by aid or if
it responds to "performance criteria"; or it may fall,
but less steeply than the growth line, as in line 2;
or it may fall more steeply, as in line 3. If the
domestic savings rate rises as the foreign savings
rate rises, the gap will be smaller: only FF_2. This
could be the result of greater private and public
efforts, or simply of the higher incomes generated
by foreign savings. A fall in the domestic savings
rate may result from increased foreign capital either
because domestic inflation leads to higher consumption
and, in real terms, reduced real investment; or because investment opportunities are thought to be
limited, so that foreign finance simply replaces
domestic finance; or because fiscal efforts to raise
public savings are relaxed. The analysis could be
carried into the political sphere. The argument
would then be that foreign support enables a government to remain in power which is unwilling to, or
incapable of, carrying out the structural reforms to
raise the savings rate.

If the domestic savings rate falls as in line
2, a sufficient increase in foreign savings to F_3
will still achieve 6 percent, but it will be more
than is suggested by the crude gap because the domestic
reduction in savings efforts has to be offset. This
is the situation that is sometimes described as
"drowning" a country in aid. But if the situation
is as in line 3, additional foreign savings can make
the growth prospect only worse and the way to achieve
6 percent may be to reduce foreign funds.

The supply of foreign savings may in turn be a
function of domestic savings (e.g., when performance
criteria are applied seriously). In this case the
EF line will be positively sloped and the equilibrium
point of intersection E can be shifted to the target
rate of growth only through bargaining and agreed
changes determining the bahavior of the curves.

This formal presentation may clarify one aspect
of the dispute between the aid and the anti-aid
lobby, even though it is grossly oversimplified and

exceedingly crude.*   Foreign savings must be scruti-
nized for the terms on which they are supplied.
Domestic savings should be an expression intended to
cover all, and only, developmental expenditure, which
includes a good deal of what is normally classified
as consumption (health, nutrition, education) and
excludes resources saved and invested in projects
which make no contribution to development.   Growth
rates are imperfect and misleading indexes of development.   Capital/output ratios have limited value.
And so on.   But the lack of a relationship between
aid and development remains even if we count aid
net of repayments or in terms of the grant element
and if we use any other development indicator, such
as greater equality, more employment, proportion of
the labor force in industry, etc.

The point which the figure makes is that special
attention must be paid to the net contribution of
aid to development, allowing for increases or relaxa-
tions of domestic efforts, both private and public,
including changes in attitudes and institutions.   In
calculating the resource gap, all forms of capital
inflow are aggregated and added to domestic savings.
But just as in trade gap calculations, export receipts
have a significance different from loans and grants,
so in resource gap calculations, private capital
differs from official capital granted or lent on
concessional terms.   The two are often complementary,
even at the margin, for a number of reasons:

-----

*Perhaps the figure raises more questions than
it answers.   Implicit in the presentation is the argument that while there may be no positive correlation
between aid and growth, growth is positively correlated
to the investment/income ratio.   But the evidence
shows only very weak correlation.   It might therefore
be the absence of a relation between investment and
growth which accounts for the absence of a relation
between aid and growth.   Further, the data of the
critics are taken mostly from cross-national studies.
The time series for particular countries might show
stronger correlations.

feasibility, design, and preinvestment studies make
private investment possible and profitable. Social
overhead such as roads, harbors, utilities, housing,
and education provide the basis for profitable private
enterprise. Soft public loans make it possible to
service private debt and private equity investment.
Aid may be necessary to help host governments to buy
out foreign capital or to prevent foreign ownership
from exercising depressing effects on local entrepreneurship. Hence filling a given aggregate gap has
a very different significance according to the composition of finance between private and public capital.

While the relation between aid and growth is
tenuous, the Pearson Report says that there is "a
close link between growth and import capacity ...
all the fast growers in the developing world received
substantial amounts of foreign financing of all
kinds. . . ."* It does not make it clear what items
are intended to be covered by "importing capacity."
A link between import capacity and aid does not re-
veal which is cause and which effect, or whether
there is mutual causation, or whether both are effects
of a third factor. Fast growth could lead to high
rates of growth of exports and could attract foreign
capital, thereby raising import capacity; or import
capacity may provide the foreign exchange which is
used to promote growth; or both causal links may be
at work; or entrepreneurial ability or high investment
may cause both. Unless we know the direction of the
causal link, no conclusions can be drawn for aid
policy. Many of the criticisms which we have made
of the resource gap apply, mutatis mutandis, to the
trade gap.

The trade (or foreign exchange) gap assumes,
misleadingly, that aid, trade, and private foreign
investment are substitutes in the provision of finance
for development. But this is not so. First, aid on
concessionary terms provides additional resources;
trade and private finance do not in themselves do

------

*Pearson et al., op. cit., p. 50.

so. Aid and private finance provide additional resources now; trade does not. Trade converts domestic
into foreign resources and may thereby raise national
income. It is remunerative if the alternative domestic
employment of the resources absorbed in exports shows
lower productivity. The second difference is that
trade raises income and domestic savings, and therefore reduces foreign exchange requirements below
what they would have been, had the same amount been
received through aid. An increase in trade therefore
removes the basis on which the gap is calculated.
Third, the effects of trade, aid, and private foreign
investment on skills and technical knowledge are
different. Only if imports are required in fixed
proportions in the production of national output and
cannot be supplied from domestic resources can a
situation arise as pictured in Figure 2, where E
shows the amount of foreign exchange available and
the distance from GG shows the dominant trade gap.

It can be seen that a reduction in domestic
savings in response to an inflow of foreign savings
now may not affect the trade gap, or it may, depending
on the location of point E and the slope of the
function.*

It may be said that all the above discussion is
beside the point. The function of gap projections
is not to analyze but to pressurize. Any self-respect-
ing country must draft its national plan so that a
gap appears which it can then ask to be filled with
foreign capital. The World Bank, members of aid
consortia, partners of consultative groups, and
bilateral donors ask to have "needs" and "requirements"

----

*It might, of course, be argued that extra aid
merely replaces other forms of foreign exchange
receipts and, in particular, exports. This would
be one way of accounting for the absence of a relation
between import capacity and growth. The impact of
aid on import capacity would always be negligible
because it would be canceled out by offsetting movements of other credit items.

served up in a pseudo-scientific form. If a first
draft of a plan does not yield a gap, the growth
rate can always be raised until the coefficients of
the Harrod-Domar mechanics produce a plausible gap.
This gap should be large enough to exploit fully all
possible capital provisions, but small enough not to
look utopian.

In spite of the above criticisms, the gap approach
has a certain merit, if its limitations are borne in
mind. Underdevelopment is tantamount to inflexibility,
immobility, and inability to coordinate the numerous
activities which have to be planned simultaneously.
For these reasons, progress in development is therefore often held up by specific bottlenecks, though
these are not always measurable in terms of financial
or even physical resources. But insofar as external
resources can break these bottlenecks, whether they
take the form of raw materials and spare parts, of
fuel and power, or of certain skills, they can contribute a multiple of their nominal value to economic
growth. Insofar as gap analysis identifies these
structural imbalances and bottlenecks, it serves a
useful purpose, though the essence of the exercise
is to get away from macroeconomic aggregates and to
identify specific needs. It is also in those circumstances that the foundations for ability to service
debts are laid. Contrariwise, projects which inflict
high recurrent costs, deprive the rest of the economy
of scarce factors, or discourage the growth of indigenous factors, are to be avoided, for they aggravate
the structural imbalances which impede progress.

In the African context the gap approach is often
replaced by an approach which emphasizes the limited
absorptive capacity of African countries for capital
assistance and occasionally even for technical assistance. "Absorptive capacity" is a concept which
appeals to the instincts of donors. It saves money
and thought. But it is an exceedingly nebulous concept. It is hardly more useful than the concept of
the "gap."

Sometimes it is used as if it implied a zero
marginal productivity of capital, so that additional

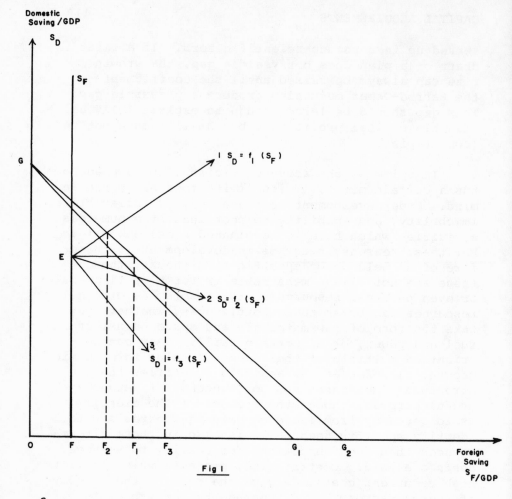

Fig 1

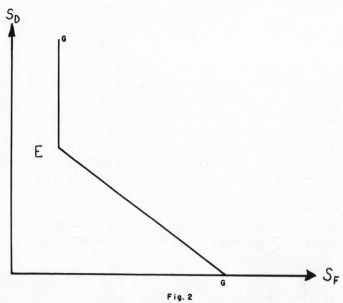

Fig. 2

foreign assistance would yield no returns. Sometimes
this is rationalized by assuming not a maximum level
of investment but a maximum investment/income ratio.
Even if the marginal productivity of investment were
zero, it would not constitute a case against additional
assistance, which could be used to subsidize consumption. In a vaguer sense, lack of "absorptive
capacity" may refer to delays or absence of suitable
projects. But such delays in loan applications or
loan disbursements or absence of suitable projects
or inefficiencies in the execution of projects may
be the fault of donors' terms and conditions, or they
may be the result of inadequate technical assistance
in project preparation and loan negotiation, or they
may be due to inadequate administration and management.

In an even more general sense, "absorptive capacity" refers to a wide range of presuppositions of
effective planning and policy-making. It covers
surveys and knowledge of available physical and human
resources; and identification of specific bottlenecks
of finance, manpower, skills, and foreign exchange;
identification of priorities and the design of a
balanced, properly phased development program, with
consistent programs for sectors. Moving down to the
project level, it implies not only sound project
selection, preparation, and presentation but also
efficient execution and assessment, so that faults
can be identified and avoided in future. It also
suggests a careful weighing of the costs of particular
strategies and a planning framework. Interpreted
in this wider sense, "absorptive capacity" means
much more than careful project identification,
selection, and preparation. It implies that the
projects themselves are part of a well-designed development strategy, that they are properly phased,
fit well into sectoral advance and mutually support
one another, and that errors are identified and
corrected.

It is clear that many African countries lack
"absorptive capacity" in this sense; but so do many
highly developed and sophisticated countries with
considerably greater reserves of skilled manpower,
administrative talent, and experience.

For the purposes of a narrower working definition
of "absorptive capacity," it is important to note
that absorptive capacity is a function of the form
of aid. Certain forms of technical and capital assistance can raise absorptive capacity. While there
are, of course, limits to absorbing knowledge and
skills, these limits depend upon the composition and
quality of technical assistance. "Absorptive capacity" also depends on the composition of aid as between project and program aid.

Concretely, "absorptive capacity" depends on
the rate at which the required number of entrepreneurs,
production engineers, managers, foremen, designers,
accountants, agronomists, health workers, teachers,
etc. can be made to grow. "Absorptive capacity" is
therefore continually changing.

The use of the misleading concept "absorptive
capacity" has served as a convenient rationalization
for limiting aid to Africa and, even more, for
limiting thinking about the required types of aid.
Instead of asking by what extra technical assistance
and improved preparation, selection, and management
of projects they can raise the productivity of investment and other development projects, donors have
rested content in telling themselves and one another
that the "absorptive capacity" of African countries
was strictly limited and that therefore more aid
was not needed.

If the intention is to design an effective policy
for international cooperation, it is necessary to
identify jointly shortages, bottlenecks, and needs
and to see how these can be overcome, broken, and
met. A blanket term like "absorptive capacity" con-
ceals rather than reveals the strategic problems.

11

THE NEED
TO PLAN
DEVELOPMENT
PLANNING

Note: I owe many ideas in this section to Lord Balogh. This study was written before the publication of the Jackson Report.*

There are two sets of constraints on the expansion of aid beyond a certain point, even if the political will and the resources are present: constraints on the capacity of donor organizations to expand and constraints on the side of the recipient to absorb additional aid. Both sets of constraints are some-times used as a convenient excuse for not raising the aid volume. But however strong the political will to give more aid, organizational limitations and limited absorptive capacity no doubt can constitute obstacles to the growth of aid in the short run. A discussion of the nature of these barriers and the best methods of breaking them down is therefore in order.

CAPACITY LIMITATIONS

One sometimes hears the expression of a desire to increase the contributions to multilateral aid

---

*A Study of the Capacity of the United Nations Development System (New York: United Nations, 1970)

agencies, if only they were capable of administering
additional aid effectively. Is it possible to identify the forces that, in the short run, limit multilateral capacity to use extra aid effectively?

Organizations need competent staff. It would
be pointless to cry out for more geniuses, for these
are inevitably scarce. It is the test of a good
organization that it gets the best out of the competent man, not that it has to rely on geniuses.
The brilliant can overcome the fetters of bad organizations. But a good organization will be able to
attract its share of the top people and, once these
are attracted, the organization will improve and
will continue to attract good people, and so on.

Problems of staffing can be subdivided into
recruiting, training, keeping, and using staff.

Recruitment

The eventual aim of international organizations
in recruitment must be to get rid of the nationality
quotas, which militate against both efficiency and
international loyalty, and move toward an open, competitive international civil service in which merit
alone counts. It is those organizations which have
come nearest to this principle that have proved most
effective in the aid field.

Training

Training is a form of investment which absorbs
some of the scarcest resources, both in terms of
time and physical resources spent on training the
trainers, and in terms of the time forgone in actual
work of the trainees. It is therefore essential to
make it as effective and render its returns as high
as possible.

The main fault of the present system of experts
is that while many of them are technically competent,
some of them have blinkers which prevent them from
seeing the technical problems in the social, political,

and cultural setting to which they have to be adapted.
Highly expert in their own subjects, they sometimes
know little about the specific problems of the societies to which they are sent. This has been one of
the main reasons why technical assistance has in
the past often failed to take root, why reports and
recommendations have been shelved, and why foreign
experts have not always been held in the highest
esteem. In order to remedy this situation, experts
must be trained in social sensitivity and in the
particular problems and their interrelations in the
countries to which they are sent. The separation
into specialized agencies has tended to strengthen
the technocratic bias and has prevented the treatment
of development as an integrated process.

Training programs of the kind run by the United
National Institute for Training and Research (UNITAR)
for resident representatives, subregional officers,
and experts would involve a very special blend of
training in tecniques, sensitivity, and communication,
and would draw on both academic research and practical
experience. Here is a field in which there is a
scope for cooperation between academic scholars and
experienced UN and IBRD officials. It is important
to combine research with training at these institutes,
for the courses must be absolutely up-to-date and
draw on current scientific, economic, and social
research. But they must also have a clear practical
orientation. My own view would be that the need,
in solving most specific development problems, to
draw on a large number of diverse disciplines makes
it advisable to locate the institutes or courses at
large centers of academic research, so that faculties
of engineering, agriculture, medicine, forestry, and
biology can be drawn upon as required. But there
may be political reasons for preferring a number of
smaller institutes at small centers or entirely independent of universities. On the other hand, it
may be most economical to reorganize and strengthen
existing institutions and courses.

PLANNING COOPERATION

Present political and institutional arrangements
militate doubly against international cooperation:

donor agencies are divided by functions and compete
for allocations of central funds without regard to
maximum effectiveness of the total, and recipient
countries are fragmented by national boundaries which
cut across and prevent rational subregional development planning. Bilateral donors have achieved a
measure of cooperation among themselves but are still
in many respects competing with one another, rather
than cooperating in achieving maximum development.
The multilateral agencies might be thought to have
as their objective the overcoming of the obstacles created by bilateral competition, but they were designed
for entirely different purposes at San Francisco. The
division by function--education, agriculture, health,
and recently industry--and the links with the respec-
tive national ministries again cut across lines
which ought to be sewn together in the process of
development planning. Deliberately planned development was not a main objective of most of the UN
agencies when they were founded, and the imposition
of this growing task upon an organizational structure
unintended for and unsuited to it has given rise to
stresses and strains. The rational solution would
be a single unified development agency which would
approach developing societies as social systems:
agricultural diversification would lead to industrialization; industrialization to urbanization, transport,
and location of industry; the construction of infrastructure would be dependent on the total plan;
there would be no division between agriculture,
health, nutrition, and education, for only an integrated approach to these problems can prevent such
counterdevelopmental reactions as the depopulation
of the countryside, which followed the growth of
primary education; health measures would be accompanied
by population policy; rural education, rural reform,
and rural public works would be combined; and so on.
Development would be treated as a complex of inter-
connected problems, and policies would take the
form of a concerted and appropriately phased attack
on several fronts.

Instead of such an integrated, coordinated
approach, the UN organizations, in spite of some

progress, still encourage fragmentation, separation,
and autonomy, with each agency stressing the technical
aspects of its contribution, without too much regard
to the social, cultural, political, and economic
setting in which these measures are to take root.

A number of cooperative programs between the
agencies and between the UNDP and the World Bank and
some of the agencies have tried to remedy these
faults; much more can be done in this direction.

There is a corresponding fragmentation on the
recipients' side. Countries' boundaries are defined
by historical, political, and administrative needs,
not by ecological, ethnological, linguistic, or
economic principles. In West Africa, planning which
would follow geographical and ecological criteria
would run east-west, along the coastal regions, the
forests and the savannahs, while the national boundaries run from north to south, cutting across the
lines of rational ecological cooperation.

National separatism is encouraged by the World
Bank's requirement of national development plans,
which do not always take into account the plans of
other countries. As individual laissez-faire in the
nineteenth century, so uncoordinated national planning
in the twentieth century leads to waste. The ECA
and the ADB have tried heroically to reduce this
waste and to encourage regional and subregional integration, but the political forces supporting these
attempts are weak or absent.

The remedy consists in decentralizing the planning
process from the headquarters of the specialized
agencies to the regions and subregions, where it
would be approached as a total process in which education, agriculture, health, nutrition, labor, and
industry are not separated as pressure groups backed
by ministries. Development planning should be de-
centralized into subregional offices corresponding
to those organized by the regional commissions of
the United Nations. This would represent an economy
of staffing, and the offices would be able to attract
good people. These offices should be responsible

either to the UNDP and the IBRD directly, or to the
ECA. The subregional planning agencies would be
staffed by trained experts and tightly controlled by
the UNDP and ADB subregional resident representatives.
These would maintain contact with the Ministries of
Finance and planning agencies of the governments in
the subregion, with the UNDP and the ADB and with
the specialized agencies as the sources of expert
advice.

While plans and projects would be elaborated at
the subregional level, reports would go back to a
central allocating committee at the Bank and the UNDP.
Allocations of funds and experts should then be made
centrally, but drawing on the knowledge of the subregional and national resident representative of the
UNDP and of the headquarters of the UN specialized
agencies. The specialized agencies would participate
in, but not control the planning of, "their" sectors.
But they would remain responsible for executing and
supervising the projects in this field.

Once a project has been approved as part of a
national or subregional plan, it is for the specialized
agencies to recruit the staff required to implement
it. The selection of experts should rest with the
headquarters of the specialized agencies. In selecting
and training experts, what was said above should be
borne in mind.

Finally, the supervision of operations in this
field should once again be administered by the subregional offices, headed by resident representatives
trained to view development as a social process and
able to communicate this knowledge. This would
relieve the present pressure on the headquarters of
the specialized agencies.

If such a set of reforms were carried out, many
of the objections to channeling more aid through
multilateral organizations would fall to the ground.
Small donor countries, eager to increase their aid
through multilateral channels, would no longer have
reasons to hesitate and large donor countries would
no longer have an excuse to starve these organizations
of funds.

While such reforms would remove obstacles, they could not in themselves generate the motive power for more assistance being channeled through the multilateral agencies. Powerful attractions for continuing bilateral aid will remain. But the multilateral attractions could be further increased by the establishment of an African Development Fund with soft loans for multinational, subregional projects.

INTERNATIONAL LIQUIDITY
AND THE LINK
BETWEEN
SPECIAL DRAWING RIGHTS
AND AID

Less developed countries are now assured of additional reserves in the form of special drawing rights (SDRs). The amount for Africa is very small and is determined by an irrelevant criterion, quotas in the IMF. In arguing for a more ample provision of international reserves, two points arise: do African LCDs need such reserve? are they able and willing to hold them?

As regards the question of need, the argument that can be made in favor of African LDCs is simple and strong. They suffer at least as much as the advanced countries from fluctuations in their balances of payments, and they therefore have an equal or greater need of additional reserves in relation to trade. This is particularly true of the African countries whose exports are concentrated on a few primary products which are liable to violent price fluctuations originating on the side of demand, and which form a large proportion of their total production. African developing countries are also, by most relevant measures, typically smaller than advanced countries or other LDCs. Since there are economies of scale in holding reserves, reserves needs, expressed as a proportion of imports, are greater. The adjustment process is likely to work more slowly and, if speeded up, more painfully. The costs of adjustment are likely to be higher because they are more specialized in production, because they

are less flexible, because factors are less mobile,
and because they do not normally export capital.
Finally, African LDCs have less access to credit
facilities and for this reason, too, need to hold
larger reserves than countries with better access to
credit. The reserves of many African LDCs are clearly
inadequate to satisfy these needs. The social benefits of reserves will also tend to be higher than in
rich countries. These benefits reflect the damage
countries can avoid by holding reserves. Underutilization of industrial capacity or stagnation caused
by import restrictions or deflation disrupts economic
development and can inflict considerable damage.

When we come to the ability and willingness of
the LDCs to hold additional reserves for periods of
need, there is more room for argument. There is
little evidence that actual reserves reflect needs.
Professor Machlup has investigated the relationship
between official reserves and imports, variations in
foreign trade, imports and capital flows, past deficits, domestic money supply, and current liabilities--
all of which may be thought to reflect need.* He
found, perhaps not altogether surprisingly, that no
systematic relationship existed. But this is true
for both poor and rich countries. It is often said
that if the LDCs were given additional reserves, they
would increase their overseas expenditure correspondingly so that their reserve levels would rapidly
revert to what they were before the reform. The conclusion is drawn that whatever may be the need of
the LDCs for greater reserves, it would be futile
to give them more than a small increase. However,
the account of the behavior of the LDCs on which
this argument rests is not confirmed by the facts.
If it were correct, the total reserves of the LDCs
would be continually tending to a minimal level; and
even if at certain periods (e.g., commodity prices
boom) they reached a higher level, they would very
rapidly fall again. In fact, the LDCs as a group

_____

*Banca Nazionale del Lavoro Quarterly Review,
No. 78 (September, 1966).

keep substantial reserves, even if oil producers are
excluded. In total, their holdings in 1968 represented
35.6 percent of their imports for the year, compared
with 32.2 percent for the Ten excluding the United
States and 34.2 percent for the United States. The
ratios of most African countries are above the LDC
and the developed country average.

The changes in liquidity of nineteen African
states between 1960 and 1970 are set out in Table 22;
ten of these countries registered an increase in
reserves and nine a reduction. Fourteen of the nineteen countries registered a fall in the ratio of
their reserves to annual imports, although some of
it may be attributed to excess reserve holdings in
1960. If we aggregate the reserves of the whole
group (excluding oil-producing Libya), the losses of
$907.9 million outweigh considerably the gains of
$458.8 million. The evidence does not, however,
show that countries are incapable of holding or re-
constituting reserves.

It is true that there are some LDCs which have
low reserves and whose propensity to spend money for
development purposes is so great that they would be
unlikely to retain in their reserves a large proportion
of any increase in liquidity that they received.
But there is no warrant in the recorded facts for
regarding this as in any sense a typical or average
African LDC behavior. All that can reasonably be
said is that if an addition is made to LDC reserves,
the ultimate effect on their reserve levels will be
somewhat less than the initial increment. On the
basis of past experience, however, this could equally
be said of many advanced countries. It can also be
argued that it is in the nature of unconditional
liquidity that its owner may either spend or hold
it. It is inherent in the nature of reserves that
they can be run down and thus finance a higher level
of expenditure than would otherwise have been possible.
In those LDCs where the ratio of reserves to imports
has fallen, this has often been the result of the
combination of an initially adequate level of reserves
with a growing volume of imports. The growth of
imports has not itself been especially large; it has

TABLE 22

International Liquidity Position of Selected
African Countries, 1960 and 1970

Country	Million $: End of Period			Percent Ratio of Reserves to Annual Imports	
	Liquidity 1960	Position 1970	Change in Reserves	1960	1970
Congo (Kinshasa)	63.0	185.0	+122.0	35.2	45.1[b]
Dahomey	8.9[a]	15.5	+6.6	28.7	16.7[c]
Ethiopia	52.7	71.2	+18.5	62.0	41.3
Ghana	278.0	71.0	-197.0	76.6	20.4[b]
Ivory Coast	34.0[a]	105.0	+71.0	28.3	27.0
Kenya	51.5[d]	219.8	+168.3	16.2[d,e]	55.3[e]
Libya	82.4	1590.1	+1507.7	48.8	287.0
Mali	11.0[a]	1.0	-10.0	68.8	1.9[c]
Mauritania	6.1	3.2	-2.9	61.0	24.5[d]
Morocco	206.0	141.0	-165.0	50.0	20.5
Niger	7.6[a]	18.8	+11.2	54.3	4.6[c]
Nigeria	434.0	244.0	-210.0	71.7	21.1
Senegal	76.0[a]	22.0	-54.0	44.1	11.3
Somalia	9.3	18.4[f]	+9.1	31.0	29.5[d]
Sudan	167.0	22.0	-145.0	91.2	7.6
Togo	7.3[a]	35.4	+28.1	28.1	53.6
Tunisia	85.0	58.0	-27.0	44.5	19.0
UAR	264.0	167.0	-97.0	39.5	34.6
Upper Volta	12.0[a]	36.0	+24.0	42.8	50.0[c]

Note: International liquidity position = gold + IMF reserve position + foreign exchange + special drawing rights.

[a]1962.
[b]1969.
[c]1967.
[d]1966.
[e]Excluding trade with Uganda and Tanzania.
[f]November, 1970.

Source: United Nations, Monthly Bulletin of Statistics.

in fact been considerably smaller, in general, than
the growth of imports in advanced countries. Such
a situation does not suggest a shortage of reserves
due to profligacy but, rather, an inability to raise
reserves in the face of growing import requirements.

The main advantage of the "link" between SDRs
and additional aid is that it makes it possible for
donors to increase aid without the anxiety about
their reserves which existed before the creation of
SDRs. This fear has been a powerful force restricting
the growth of aid and worsening its terms. In particular, it has led to tying and thus has reduced the
value of aid. The link might also meet the points
of those countries which feel unable to make budgetary
appropriations for more aid because it would make it
possible to give more aid without this appearing in
the budget. While this might overcome budgetary constraints of a political nature, it clearly would not
affect the need to take fiscal measures to combat
inflation, if the impact were inflationary. Furthermore, it would meet the widespread desire of many
developed countries to generate export surpluses in
exchange for reserves and would therefore improve
the general international monetary situation. The
creation of additional liquidity should therefore
be linked with the provision of additional capital
aid to Africa.

The Board of Governors of the IMF in Rio de
Janeiro in 1967 agreed on a scheme of SDRs which was
activated in 1970. A recent group of experts endorsed
the recommendation of the first UNCTAD expert group
and showed the technical feasibility of linking SDRs
with development aid.* The group had among its members
distinguished German, French, and Belgian representatives, as well as members from Britain, the United
States, the USSR, Hungary, and the developing countries.

_____

*International Monetary Reform and Cooperation
for Development, E. 70 II. D.2 (1969).

Prima facie, the adoption of such a proposal
would be of considerable advantage to the developing
countries. They would, at least initially, obtain
a substantial accretion in the flow of development
aid on easy terms. (It could be on easy terms, since
there would be no necessity for the IMF to charge
the IDA more than a "moderate rate of interest,"
perhaps 1.5 percent per year, on the SDRs or equivalent currencies transferred.) International monetary
reserves are now about $70,000 million. An increase
in international liquidity of $3,500 million in the
first year and $3,000 million in the two subsequent
years is envisaged. This is about 5 percent of total
reserves per year. Part I members of IDA receive
$2,300 million per year over the next three years.
If the 70 percent, which there is no obligation to
reconstitute, were distributed to IDA, this would
yield $1,600 million per year a fourfold increase in
IDA resources and a substantial amount in relation
to the current world flow in aid. At the same time,
it would be little more than one half per mil of
the demand for output in OECD countries, which amounted
to $1,700 billion in 1968.

Taking a wider point of view, the case for the
link is that it would enable a generally agreed-upon
objective--the increase in the flow of aid to the
LDCs--to be achieved while safeguarding the donor
countries against the danger, which most of them fear,
that increased aid will damage their international
liquidity position. That there is widespread fear
of the effect of aid on the balance of payments is
shown by the prevalence of tying. Even countries
with strong reserves and persistent surpluses tie
their aid (thereby increasing the inflationary pressures whose effects on their economies they continually
bemoan). Any aid given via the link mechanism will
carry with it a built-in guarantee, for the donor
countries as a whole, against a loss of reserves.
Further, the greater the extent to which one advanced
country makes real resources available to the LDCs
through the link, the greater the extent to which
it will share in the ultimate distribution of reserves.

These considerations are of particular importance
to any country which has emphasized that the volume

of its aid is restricted by balance of payments considerations substantially below the level which it
should otherwise like to see it attain. That they
are relevant to such a large part of the whole field
of aid has a bearing on one argument which is often
used in criticism of the link proposal: the assertion
that monetary reform and increasing aid are logically
separate objectives which can and should be separately
pursued. The fact is that concern about national
balances of payments, which is a symptom of a world
economy suffering from liquidity shortage, is also
a powerful constraint upon and inhibitor of aid
policy. And from a practical point of view, though
it is true that any international monetary reform
which brings about a general increase in liquidity
will tend to cause a liberalization of aid policies,
it is exceedingly doubtful whether this process would
in a long time, or indeed ever, have the same effect
on the flow of aid as would a scheme which linked
the two things together right from the start. To
put the same point another way, it may be true that
if a link proposal were adopted, some donors would
say that the existence of this new aid channel made
it unnecessary for them to go on giving so much
directly and would reduce the scale of their bilateral
aid. But it seems not unlikely, for practical reasons
and because of the changed aspect of the balance of
payments problem, that this could produce more than
a fairly small offset to the direct effect of the
proposal on the volume of capital aid.

There is another reason for expecting that the
link proposal would lead to an increase in the total
flow of aid. This is that it provides an automatic
and unquestioned method of sharing the burden of the
additional aid. It thus avoids the disputes about
burden sharing which have tended to occur in international aid operations (especially in the discussions
of replenishing IDA) and which tend to make any such
operations small-scale and slow-moving.

The adoption of the link would not only increase
the total flow of aid: it would also lead to a higher
proportion of the flow being channeled through IDA
if this method were adopted. This must be reckoned
as a considerable advantage, implying better

administration of the aid on average and better value
in relation to the aid given--probably quite a lot
better.   But it would be possible to attach the link
to any other scheme.   Thus monetary reform could be
linked with supplementary financial measures, the
scheme which proposes to insure LDCs against unexpected
shortfalls in export earnings, or with debt relief
or with commodity schemes or buffer stock financing
or with regional development banks.

From the point of view of Africa, there would
be merit in pressing for contributions of SDRs or
the equivalent currencies to the African Development
Fund, if it were to be a soft-loan window of the
African Development Bank.   A portion of SDRs might
also be used to contribute to the reserves of subregional or regional payments unions if these were
considered helpful to promote regional integration.

It seems clear, therefore, that the adoption of
the link would bring substantial economic advantages
to the LDCs.   We have next to consider whether, and
to what extent, this gain to the LDCs would be matched
by a "loss" or cost to the advanced deficit country
is conceivable that an advanced deficit country might
find itself in the position of not earning extra
SDRs or having to buy back its own currency from
an advanced surplus country, on whose exports the
SDRs or currency had been spent, and so of failing
to share in the liquidity gain.   At worst, the country concerned might be no better off in terms of
total liquidity than it was before the creation of
SDRs.

Deficit countries with balance of payments
problems might thus increase their reserves by raising
their development orders, and surplus countries with
budgetary problems might increase their aid, without
budgetary appropriations.   In both cases, of course,
additional real resources would have to be made available, although these would be small in relation to
total national product.

Some of the advanced countries might not find
the effect of the proposal so much to their taste

as others. They would see it as facing them with
the prospect of increased pressure of demand on their
economies, which are already overemployed and suffering
from inflation. They could avoid this only by not
taking any share in the new development orders; and
if they did this, they would not gain any of the
additional liquidity created through the link. It
is clear that it would not be reasonable for a country to support the proposal unless it was prepared
to make an additional transfer of real resources in
favor of the LDCs. If it is so prepared, however,
it should also be willing to take action to reduce
domestic demand to the extent necessary to prevent
an overloading of the economy. Clearly, the proposal
has no chance of being adopted unless there is a
sufficient number of countries who are willing to
make a greater real transfer to the LDCs so long as
their balances of payments and reserve positions are
safeguarded. If this is the case, then the difficulty
about inflationary pressure, which in any case is
likely to be very small, is not insuperable. And
the need to earn reserves, in exchange for real resources, should provide a safeguard against excessive
expansion of reserve assets and should appeal to
those concerned by the inflationary dangers of the
link.

An objection which has been made to the link
proposal is related to the time pattern of the two
operations which it is desired to link. This point
is stated as follows by the Ossola Report:

> From the point of view of international
> monetary management, full flexibility of
> decision is called for as to whether assets
> should be created or not. From the point
> of view of development, on the other hand,
> planning both by donors and by recipients
> requires firm commitments over consider-
> able periods. This would introduce an in-
> flexibility into the monetary aspects of
> the scheme and thus impair the monetary
> quality of the asset.*

---

*Group of Ten, Report of the Study Group on the

As was stated above, this criticism may apply
to the Stamp proposal but has little substance as
applied to the experts' proposal. Under their scheme
the volume, timing, and distribution of SDRs would
be determined by the estimated needs of the world
economy, not by development needs. A proportion of
these newly created SDRs would be put at the disposal
of IDA, and the size and timing of this provision
would be designed to meet the needs of development
policy. It should be possible to achieve quite a
satisfactory degree of continuity from the point of
view of IBRD/IDA planning; indeed, the situation
with "link" finance might well be an improvement on
the types of finance available to the IBRD for financing IDA at the moment.

It is a common objection to the link that liquidity and aid are entirely separate problems which
cannot and should not be packaged together. If a
group of countries--the argument runs--wish to give
each other credit, or create additional liquidity
for one another, there is no reason why they should
not be entitled to create the necessary instruments
for themselves without linking this scheme with the
provision of real resources to LDCs. The reply to
this argument (given by Professor Machlup) is that
the creation of new liquidity presents a saving compared with the acquisition of gold. When new gold
deposits were discovered, those who wished to acquire
gold had to give up real resources. The introduction
of international "paper" money amounts to a technical
invention which saves resources. It is sensible and
it is just that this saving should accrue to those
most in need, the LDCs, and that richer countries
should have to earn at least part of it.

There remains the question as to the most suitable
form for the link. Ultimately, when the stock of
international liquidity has been adequately augmented
(if it continues at the present rate, it will double

Creation of Reserve Assets (Washington, D.C.:   IMF,
1965), p. 70.

in twenty years), the IMF might issue the SDRs directly
to the LDCs according to an agreed formula. The industrial countries would have to earn them in precisely
the same manner in which they had to earn gold until
recently, by additional exports. The only difference
would be that the earnings would accrue to those engaged in development rather than those in whose moun-
tains a metal happened to be buried. But until confidence in SDRs has been established and reserves
have grown to an adequate level, the channeling will
have to be done through international organizations
and careful attention will have to be paid that the
aims of liquidity creation and development aid are
kept strictly separate.

For the present there are two possibilities:
an "organic" and a "nonorganic" link. In an "organic"
link SDRs are themselves allocated to the IDA, which
in turn uses them or national currencies to extend
development loans. In a "nonorganic" link, international liquidity creation would be accompanied by
voluntary pledging, either once-for-all or repeatedly,
of all Part 1 member countries of IDA of a uniform
proportion of their newly acquired SDRs to the IDA.
The difficulty about an organic link is that the
Articles of Agreement of the IMF, as now amended,
rule out the holdings of SDRs by multilateral institutions engaged in development assistance. A re-
negotiation of these Articles is arduous at this
stage. It may, however, still be preferable to the
alternatives. The difficulty about the nonorganic
link is that it may run into problems of national
appropriation procedure or of national legislation
of other kinds. Either course runs into difficulties,
and the expert group recommended that the course
should be chosen which seems politically feasible.

It may be finally argued that the attempt to
forge a link between SDRs and aid may weaken the
confidence that needs to be built up for SDRs and
the success of international monetary reform is of
much greater importance to the LDCs than the link.
It is also said that the link may reduce the chances
of increasing bilateral and multilateral aid in more
conventional ways. These objections raise problems

of strategy and tactics. Even if the link were to
reduce other flows of aid, the total is likely to be
larger and of better quality. Nurturing confidence
in SDRs is more important than the link. But favoring
the link need not reduce the chances of success of
the SDR scheme or of an increase in conventional forms
of aid.

From this discussion of the probable consequences
of adopting the "link" proposal the following conclusions emerge:

1. The adoption of the proposal would in practice probably result in (a) a large total volume of
aid; (b) a higher proportion of aid channeled through
the IDA and therefore to Africa, or to the African
Development Fund, with consequential gain in quality;
(c) an opportunity for donors to earn reserves by
meeting export orders, at some cost in diversion of
resources to aid from domestic use, where such resources are already fully employed.

2. It is not true that there is any necessary
conflict between the timing of the monetary operation
and that of the provision of development finance.

3. The fear of inflation has not much justification. If in a particular country exports were to
create inflationary pressures, the country, if willing
to give more aid, would take the necessary measures
to set the resources free.

The proposal thus offers an opportunity of
giving a substantial encouragement to the development
of the LDCs while safeguarding the donor countries
against any ill effects on their balance of payments
or budgetary positions. It also offers advanced
deficit countries an opportunity to strengthen their
reserve positions by making a special effort to fill
the development orders which the scheme would generate.

There are a number of variations on the link
proposal discussed above. The proposal of the Hon.
Maxwell Stamp has already been mentioned. The Stamp
plan consists in issuing SDRs to LDCs, which can

spend these for development purposes in countries
that express their willingness to accept them. The
objection to this solution is that the creation of
international reserves and its timing should be
guided by considerations other than the need for
aid. The merit of the plan of the UNCTAD experts is
that the volume, timing, and distribution of SDRs
can be guided entirely by the requirements of international liquidity; and if SDRs are immediately ex-
changed for national currencies, no conflict arises.
On the other hand, one may anticipate a future in
which international reserves will be so ample that
the delay between issue of SDRs to LDCs and acquisition
of them by developed countries will not be regarded
as a serious objection. The Scitovsky proposal meets
this objection by shifting the initiative of reserve
creation to deficit countries in need of additional
reserves and ready to surrender real resources for
aid.* A deficit country in need of reserve makes a
budgetary appropriation for grants-in-aid to LDCs
and hands over this grant to the IMF in the form of
its national currency or government debt or, alternatively, tied contribution to IDA. The IMF issues
SDRs against the security of this country's currency
or debt and makes it available to IDA. IDA gives it
to an LDC for the purpose of financing development
imports. The LDC receiving the money can spend it
only in the country against whose currency or debt
it was issued; but once in this country's hands, it
becomes unrestricted international liquidity, spendable
and acceptable anywhere. In other words, the LDC
receives a tied grant (to which not the same objections
apply as to a tied loan): the deficit country receives
additional external reserves, but only in exchange
for real resources. This proviso prevents reserves
from being too easily acquired. To link the creation

---

*Requirements of an International Reserve System,
Essays in International Finance No. 49, International
Finance Section (Princeton: Princeton University
Press, 1965), pp. 10-13; and "A New Approach to In-
ternational Liquidity," American Economic Review,
LVI, 5, December, 1966, 1212-20.

of international money to the financing of development would follow a respectable tradition: on the
national level, deposit money was created against
bank credit that helped to finance industrial development.   This proposal would not be open to the objection
that surplus countries would be exposed to additional
inflationary pressure.

13

THE PROBLEM

OF TYING

LIMITED UNTYING

The costs of tied aid to recipient countries
are now generally recognized and attempts have been
made to quantify them.* An UNCTAD Secretariat paper
estimates these costs as at least 10-20 percent.
It would be utopian to ask for complete untying of
all aid while donor countries are concerned with
their balance of payments and reserve positions. At
the same time, there are steps that should and could
be taken which combine substantial benefits to recipients with low balance of payments costs to donors.

One such step is to permit tied aid to be spent
on goods and services of other less developed countries in the region. Such limited untying would
encourage regional trade between developing countries

---

*Mahbub ul Haq, "Tied Credits--A Quantitative
Analysis," in John Adler, ed., Capital Movements and
Economic Development (New York: St. Martin's Press,
1967); D. Lal, Cost of Aid-Tying--A Case Study of
India's Chemical Industry (New York: UNCTAD, 1967);
J. Bhagwati, The Tying of Aid, TD/7/Supp. 4 (New
York: UNCTAD, 1967); and R. M. Honavar, "Aid-Tying
by Source and Industrial Efficiency" (Economic Develop-
ment Institute, IBRD 1967) (mimeographed).

and investment in them. There might be some increase
in switching because the range of products on which
switching could be exercised would have been enlarged
(i.e., purchase previously made out of earned foreign
exchange would be replaced by products bought out of
tied aid and the foreign exchange thus saved concerted), so that some donors might lose more than
under a system of strictly bilateral tying. But the
amount would be small. In addition to encouraging
regional and subregional trade and investment, such
a measure would reduce somewhat the distortions introduced by biases in favor of highly capital-intensive
and import-intensive projects.

     An objection raised to this proposal is that
African countries are not in a position to fulfill
the orders for engineering goods and other types of
aid financed products. There are two replies to
this. In the first place, the evidence shows that
the proportion of orders from the EDF which go to
the other associated states is one-quarter of the
total. This does not suggest severe supply limitations. But, second, even where supplies are not yet
available, the opportunity to meet orders provides
the growing market and the stimulus to industrial
development that is otherwise lacking.

                    RECIPROCAL UNTYING

     In addition to steps toward limited untying for
purchases from other LDCs, donors should explore the
possibility of reciprocal untying between two or more
donor countries willing to accommodate each other for
possible foreign exchange losses. It seems that the
existence of a few countries with a chronic tendency
toward balance of payments surpluses should not prevent
deficit countries from adopting measures of reciprocal
untying among themselves.

     These limited, step-by-step advances toward
more effective aid policies could be negotiated in
consultative groups or bilaterally between donors
and groups of recipients.

TAXES AND SUBSIDIES

There is another alternative to tying which combines the merits of the price mechanism with insurance
against reserve losses. This alternative would permit deficit countries, where exports would otherwise
not be competitive, to earn reserves and would permit
surplus countries to avoid the impact of inflationary
pressures. The solution is to impose indirect taxes
on the aid-financed exports of surplus countries and
to give subsidies to the aid-financed exports of
deficit countries. These would clearly apply only
to loans, for there is less objection to tying grants.
Such a system would permit otherwise noncompetitive
deficit countries to earn reserves in exchange for
real resources while insulating surplus countries
with adequate reserves, unwilling to suffer inflationary pressures, against aid-generated demand. It
would be possible to finance the subsidies nationally
and keep the receipts of the export taxes, or a multinational agency might be used as a financing organization. Here again, a certain amount of switching
would occur, recipients buying subsidized exports
out of aid loans which they would otherwise have
bought out of earned foreign exchange. But there is
bound to be some increase in purchases from deficit
donors and a reduction in those from surplus donors.

14

**THE
SPECIAL
CLAIMS
OF AFRICA**

While growth of total product and income per
head has been quite impressive between 1960 and 1967
in many developing countries. Africa has lagged
behind. Growth in all developing countries in this
period was 5 percent and growth per head 2.4 percent.
The least underdeveloped countries, i.e., those of
Europe, registered the highest growth rates (7.1 total,
5.6 per head), while Africa, which contains many of
the least developed countries, registered the lowest
growth rates (3.1 total and 0.9 per head). According
to the Survey of Economic Conditions in Africa, 1969,
total GDP grew annually by 3.3 percent between 1965
and 1968, and GDP per head by only 0.5 percent.
Income per head in some African countries actually
declined over this period. Only two African countries,
Libya and Liberia, figured among those with growth
records of 6 percent or more per annum.

This disparity of growth rates within the third
world implies that gaps in income per head are widening not only between rich and poor countries but also
between very poor and not quite so poor countries.
For it is largely those countries in which income
levels are relatively high which register higher growth
rates, while the least developed countries have been
condemned to the lowest growth rates. Africa contains
twenty-one of the twenty-seven countries with lowest
GDP per head. Of forty developing countries on the

continent, twenty-one are among those with the lowest
national income per head in the world. Thirty countries, comprising 86 percent of the population,
enjoy a GDP of less than $160 per head and seventeen
of these, with 55 percent of the population, less
than $80 per head. What insignificant growth there
was, was confined largely to mining and services,
while food production per head, on which the bulk of
the population depends, grew hardly at all or fell.

The flow per head of net official and multilateral
resources is one measure of the potential contribution
of these external flows to the development of a recipient country. There were substantial disparities in
average per capita aid inflows from developed market
economies and multilateral agencies to various developing subregions in 1960-65. The average ranged from
$2.34 (South Asia) to $12.21 (North Africa). However,
there has been a considerable narrowing of the range
of annual averages of seven subregions (North Africa,
Africa south of the Sahara, South America, North and
Central America, South Asia, Middle East, and Far
East). The decline of average annual aid per head
to North Africa from the very high levels of over
$14.00 in 1960-61 to about $8.00 in 1965 was particularly marked.[1] (Aid per head to Africa south of the
Sahara averaged under $5 per head,)[2] "In four sub-
regions with the lowest averages in 1960--South
America, South Asia, North and Central America, Africa
south of the Sahara--per capita aid increased over
the period 1960-1965".[3] The net inflow of capital
per head varies considerably between recipient countries. In 1967 nearly twenty African countries
received less than $3 per head, while eighteen re-
ceived more than $10. The evidence "suggests that
income per head is not an important influence on the
distribution of external development finance".[4]
However, it is often the lowest-income countries that
have the greatest difficulty in diversifying and
expanding their exports, and these countries are also
frequently unable to provide strong attractions to
private foreign capital. Their dependence on external
assistance is particularly great.

The low level of income and development in many
African countries has important implications for aid

policy. One is the need for a relatively large
share of technical assistance. But technical assistance requires much more careful planning and coordination than capital aid. Hence the imperative
need for the reform of the UN agencies and for the
effective organization of consultative groups.

   The geographical distribution of technical assistance in general shows two special features. First,
levels of receipts per head are not as widely spread
as those for the distribution of total aid.[5] The
major exception is that eight countries at the low
end of the scale received more than $50 worth of
technical assistance per head per year in 1965-66,
whereas the average for all countries was $0.82.[6]
Second, there seems to be a tendency for the distribution of technical assistance--and especially educational assistance--to conform to a reasonable
judgment of the urgency of needs, e.g., the average
receipts of over $2 per head in Africa, as compared
with $0.29 in Southern Europe is consistent with the
urgent African needs for operational help and the
enormous efforts being made to develop the educational
system on that continent.[7]

   Another implication of low income levels, accompanied by small size of countries, is the need
for strong regional coordination. If the African
Development Bank were able to draw on more substantial
sums of money, both from outside and from within
Africa, there would be scope for projects that would
overcome the severe limits of small and fragmented
markets resulting from low incomes and small countries.

   Most African countries gained independence
between 1955 and 1963. The transition to independence
imposed political strains and the need for larger
investment outlays on physical and social infrastructure. Such expenditures lay the foundations
for development but do not contribute to rapid increases in measured income.

   One of the declared functions of aid is to
reduce growing international inequalities. But this
principle is usually applied only to the income gap
between the developed and the developing countries.

TABLE 23

Per Capita Receipts of Net Official Assistance
by Selected Developing Countries from OECD/DAC
Countries and Multilateral Agencies, 1967-69
(annual average; U.S.$)

Recepient Area/Country	Bilateral	Multilateral	Total
Africa	4.27	0.80	5.07
Algeria	8.18	-0.09	8.10
Libya	2.56	-1.91	0.64
Morocco	5.39	0.73	6.12
Tunisia	19.21	2.27	21.48
UAR (Egypt)	0.40	0.10	0.50
Burundi	2.73	0.98	3.71
Congo (Kinshasa)	4.42	0.08	4.50
Ethiopia	1.26	0.45	1.72
Ghana	8.31	0.35	8.66
Guinea	2.04	0.69	2.73
Kenya	3.76	1.80	5.57
Liberia	19.84	1.69	21.53
Malawi	5.70	0.70	6.41
Nigeria	1.14	0.48	1.62

Rwanda	3.53	0.82	4.36
Sierra Leone	3.14	0.27	3.42
Somalia	6.16	2.61	8.78
Tanzania	2.30	0.54	2.84
Uganda	2.25	0.26	2.53
Zambia	10.55	0.01	10.56
Cameroon	4.00	2.27	6.27
Central African Republic	6.75	3.44	10.19
Chad	2.91	2.25	5.16
Congo (Brazzaville)	11.76	19.42	31.18
Dahomey	31.8	2.33	5.51
Gabon	16.27	4.73	21.00
Ivory Coast	6.81	2.14	8.96
Madagascar	3.14	2.20	5.34
Mali	1.65	1.76	3.41
Mauritania	4.04	3.26	7.31
Senegal	7.97	3.43	11.41
Togo	4.12	2.64	6.77
Upper Volta	2.37	1.10	3.48

Source: OECD, Development Assistance Review, 1970.

TABLE 24

Official Financial Flows of Aid to African Countries from
OECD/DAC Countries and Multilateral Agencies, 1965-67
(average annual disbursements net of amortization; £ sterling per capita)

Recipient (ranked by aid per capita)	Total Aid[1]	Principal Donors[2]	U.K.	U.S.	France	Germany	EEC	Japan	Other DAC[3]	Other Multi-lateral
St. Helena	90.48	U.K. 100%	90.26	0.22	--	--	--	--	--	--
Liberia	13.53	U.S. 68% Germany 26%	0.08	9.20	--	3.53	--	--	0.14	0.58
Seychelles	11.58	U.K. 98%	11.35	0.10	--	--	--	--	0.05	0.08
Swaziland	11.43	U.K. 94%	10.79	0.01	--	0.03	--	--	0.08	0.52
Gabon	9.90		0.05	0.82	3.92	0.92	2.00	--	0.03	2.22
Botswana	9.51	U.K. 82%	7.76	0.83	--	--	--	--	0.11	0.81
Tunisia	7.12	U.S. 52% France 16% Italy 12%	--	3.71	1.16	0.50	--	--	1.31	0.44
Congo (Brazzaville)	6.37	France 49% EEC 27% IBRD 8%	0.01	0.28	3.15	0.40	1.70	--	0.03	0.79
Lesotho	4.92	U.K. 86%	4.24	0.14	--	0.03	--	--	0.11	0.40
Sao Tome and Principe	3.85	Portugal 100%	--	--	--	--	--	--	3.85	...
Senegal	3.75	France 54% EEC 31%	--	0.22	2.03	0.08	1.15	--	0.06	0.21
Algeria	3.51	France 91%	--	0.41	3.18	0.02	0.07	--	0.03	(-)0.20
Central African Republic	3.38	France 58% EEC 28%	0.01	0.18	1.95	0.11	0.96	--	0.04	0.14
Zambia	3.38	U.K. 73% Italy 17%	2.46	0.49	--	0.02	--	--	0.62	(-)0.21
Gambia	3.37	U.K. 91%	3.07	0.04	--	0.19	--	--	0.04	0.02
Cape Verde	3.21	Portugal 100%	--	--	--	--	--	--	3.21	...

Country		Sources								
Ghana	3.12	U.S. 62% Germany 13% IBRD 10%	0.05	1.92	0.04	0.42	--	0.01	0.39	0.30
Ivory Coast	2.89	France 48% EEC 29% U.S. 12%	--	0.35	1.38	0.14	0.85	--	0.18	(-)0.01
Malawi	2.80	U.K. 83%	2.31	0.28	--	0.13	--	--	0.07	0.02
Somalia	2.77	U.S. 33% Italy 32% Germany 16%	--	0.92	--	0.44	0.23	--	0.89	0.29
Togo	2.52		--	0.31	0.42	1.01	0.53	--	0.05	0.20
Congo (Kinshasa)	2.45	Belgium 56% U.S. 33%	0.01	0.80	0.01	0.04	0.09	--	1.47	0.03
Morocco	2.40	U.S. 47% France 31% Germany 10%	--	1.12	0.75	0.24	--	--	0.03	0.25
Kenya	2.32	U.K. 56% U.S. 16% IBRD 11%	1.30	0.38	--	0.09	--	0.01	0.15	0.39
Dahomey	2.17	France 48% EEC 29% Italy 8%	--	0.15	1.03	0.06	0.63	--	0.22	0.08
Mauritius	2.15	U.K. 73% IBRD 16%	1.56	0.01	--	--	--	--	0.06	0.52
Madagascar	2.08	France 50% EEC 30%	--	0.07	1.05	0.23	0.62	--	0.01	0.10

Continued

Table 24 Continued

Recipient (ranked by aid per capita)	Total Aid[1]	Principal Donors[2]	U.K.	U.S.	France	Germany	EEC	Japan	Other DAC[3]	Other Multi-lateral
Cameroon	2.06	EEC 41% U.S. 15% France 29%	0.02	0.30	0.59	0.16	0.84	--	0.07	0.06
Sierra Leone	1.94	U.S. 61% U.K. 21%	0.40	1.19	--	0.13	--	--	0.04	0.18
Niger	1.83	France 50% EEC 30% U.S. 11%	--	0.21	0.91	0.08	0.54	--	0.01	0.07
Chad	1.68	France 52% EEC 27% U.S. 9%	--	0.15	0.87	0.11	0.46	--	0.02	0.06
Guinea	1.60	U.S. 86%	--	1.37	(-)0.14	0.17	--	--	0.08	0.12
Mauritania	1.53	France 76% EEC 18%	--	0.01	1.16	0.02	0.89	--	--	(-)0.55
Mali	1.36	EEC 49% France 25% U.S. 14%	--	0.19	0.34	0.04	0.66	--		0.12
Rwanda	1.27		--	0.17	0.01	0.06	0.16	--	0.82	0.04
Tanzania	1.13		0.32	0.31	--	0.14	--	--	0.25	0.10
Uganda	1.04	U.K. 58% U.S. 20% Germany 11%	0.60	0.21	--	0.11	--	--	0.06	0.06
Upper Volta	0.98	France 45% EEC 35% U.S. 11%	--	0.11	0.44	0.02	0.34	=-	0.01	0.06
Burundi	0.89	Belgium 62% EEC 15% U.S. 9%	--	0.08	0.02	0.04	0.13	--	0.56	0.06

	Col 2	Col 3	Col 4	Col 5	Col 6	Col 7	Col 8	Col 9	Col 10	Col 11
UAR	0.83	U.S. 65% Germany 14% Italy 12%	--	0.54	0.05	0.12	--	--	0.11	0.01
Angola	0.65	Portugal 97%	--	--	--	--	--	--	0.65	--
Libya	0.63	Italy 33% U.K. 25% Germany 24%	0.16	0.11	--	0.15	--	--	0.23	(-)0.03
Nigeria	0.60		0.11	0.18	--	0.05	--	--	0.08	0.18
Sudan	0.56		0.09	0.14	--	0.13	--	--	0.04	0.16
Portuguese Guinea	0.50	Portugal 100%	--	--	--	--	--	--	0.50	...
Ethiopia	0.49		0.01	0.23	--	0.05	--	--	0.07	0.14
Mozambique	0.48	Portugal 94%	0.02	--	--	--	--	--	0.46	--
Rhodesia	(-)0.11	(positive flow =£ 0.12 £ per capita; U.K. 83% of this)	0.10	--	--	--	--	--	0.02	(-)0.22

Notes: Percentages refer to total aid, i.e., positive flow less debt repayment.
A conversion rate of £1 = U.S. $2.80 was used throughout.
-- = nil or negligible.
... = not available.

1 Cols. 4-11 do not necessarily add to col. 2 due to conversion roundings.
2 Three or fewer donors providing more than 80% of col. 2.
3 Includes Australia and Switzerland.

TABLE 25

Estimated Assistance to Regions to Which French
Overseas Territories and Departments Belong

Total Aid	Region	U.K.	U.S.	France	Germany	EEC	Japan	Other DAC	Other Multilateral
41.25	Africa Comoro Is Somaliland Reunion	--	0.01	40.33	--	1.13	--	--	0.05
...	America St. Pierre et Miquelon Guadeloupe Martinique Guipna	...	...	68.87	...	...	...	...	...
56.10	Oceania French Polynesia New Caledonia Wallis and Futuna	0.01	--	53.45	--	2.59	--	--	0.05

Note: Data on French assistance to these overseas territories and departments are not available on an individual basis.

Source: OECD, Geographical Distribution of Financial Flows to Less Developed Countries.

If the principle is applied to the third world, aid
should be increasingly directed to those with the
lowest incomes and lowest development prospects, in
order to avoid growing inequalities within the group
of LDCs. Even quite apart from income differentials,
an important purpose of aid is to help those who are
poorest and most in need of assistance. On both
these grounds, the claims of many African countries
for more aid are very strong.

There is a school of thought which holds that
the aid is used most effectively when performance
criteria are applied. Then self-help measures are
rewarded and success is backed by outside support.
While this doctrine has considerable attractions,
it is important that the criteria applied to performance are correctly chosen. Growth rates of income
or of income per head can be quite misleading criteria
for this purpose.

The task in many African countries today is to
lay the human, institutional, and technical foundations
for a progressing economy. This means creating an
educational system adapted to economic growth, an
efficient and honest administrative service, a literate
and motivated class of farmers, and a disciplined,
skilled, and adaptable agricultural and industrial
labor force. It means creating financial institutions,
building up markets, and establishing communications:
roads, railways, harbors. All these are essential
conditions, but they do not result immediately in
rapid or accelerated growth rates. After a time,
however, they tend to show rapidly increasing returns.
If we accept, for the purpose of this argument,
Rostowian terminology, the required measures amount
to preparing the runway, without which "takeoff" is
impossible, but do not immediately lead to soaring
flights. Any proper application of performance
criteria must pay attention to these institution-
building and foundation-laying activities, much more
than to the behavior of aggregates like national
income, savings, investment, or growth rates.

The emphasis on helping those "nearest to takeoff," those most capable of helping themselves, is

also in blatant contradiction with the argument that
it is the purpose of aid to reduce income inequali-
ties--for such a policy would increase inequalities.

Even if the objective of aid is to minimize the
difference in the present value of the expected income stream resulting from aid and what it would be
without aid, the utility derived from income diminishes
with its size. A given difference expressed in dollars
should therefore be weighted more heavily if it accrues
to a low-income country than if it accrues to a high-
income country. Such differential weighting is entirely consistent with "maximizing the development
impact" of aid.

We conclude that lower-income countries have a
stronger claim on scarce aid funds than higher-income
countries for three quite distinct reasons.

First, there is the humanitarian claim to help
those most in need. There is greater value in helping
a lame dog over a stile than in patting an express
train as it rushes by and claiming credit for its
speed.

Second, if the objective is to reduce international income differentials, the slowest growers,
who are also often the poorest, have a stronger claim
than faster growers among the developing countries.

Third, even if the aim is pure maximization of
the development impact of aid, an interpretation in
terms of human satisfaction indicates heavier weighting
for the poorest than for less poor countries.

Table 26 shows some of the African LDCs and
some social and economic indicators. Our argument
leads to the conclusion that, within the aid total,
there is a special case for allocating aid funds
according to a separate target, to the support of
public services like health and education, and to
institution-building. The case is analogous to that
for central government grants to local authorities
for the conduct of public services. The case can
be based upon the indivisibility of the need for

TABLE 26

Some African Least Developed Countries: Economic and Social Indicators

Country	Population (million)	GNP per Head (U.S. $)	Annual Growth of Population (percent)	Annual Growth of Real GDP 1960-65 (percent)	Illiteracy (percent)	Primary and Secondary School Enrolment (percent)	Inhabitants per Doctor (thousand)	Energy Consumption per Head (Kg coal equivalent)	Proportion of GDP Originating in Manufacturing (percent)
Botswana	0.575	60	3.0	*	80	44	21	*	*
Burundi	3.27	50	2.0	*	*	18	59	12	*
Chad	3.36	70	1.5	*	95	20	73	15	4
Dahomey	2.41	80	2.9	5.0	95	20	20	30	8
Ethiopia	23.0	60	1.7	3.5	95	8	69	10	7
Gambia	0.336	90	2.0	4.7	90	18	22	39	*
Guinea	3.61	80	2.7	6.7	90	19	21	98	
Lesotho	0.865	60	2.9	*	65	76	18	*	5
Malawi	4.04	50	2.4	1.0	94	31	50	42	1
Mali	4.65	60	2.2	5.0	95	14	40	21	3
Niger	3.43	80	3.2	4.1	99	6	66	13	
Rwanda	3.20	40	3.1	*	90-95	44	97	15	7
Somalia	2.58	50	3.4	*	95	6	30	27	*
Tanzania	11.83	80	1.9	3.1	80-85	23	20	55	4
Upper Volta	4.96	50	2.5	5.0	90-95	8	64	10	1

*= not known

Note: Many of the figures are either very rough approximations or informed guesses.

Source: International Development Review, XI, 3, (September, 1969), p. 3.

certain minimum standards of health and education, so that inadequacies in one part of the world can poison and infect others. Or it can be based on humanitarian considerations of human rights. It can also be based on contributing to growth potential, for appropriate measures of health and education are not only desirable in their own right but are also forms of human investment and conducive to speeider development. It would therefore be proper to ensure that within the general aid strategy, the needs of the LDCs be given special attention, either by setting up specific targets for contribution, supported by a machinery of implementation, or by setting up programs in terms of specific objectives to be achieved, which donors agree to underwrite.

NOTES

1.   UNCTAD, Growth and External Development Finance, TD/7/Supp. 1.

2.   UNCTAD, External Development Finance: Present and Future, TD/B/C.3/61.

3.   UNCTAD, Growth and External Development Finance, TD/7/Supp. 1.

4.   Ibid.

5.   OECD, 1968 Review.

6.   Ibid.

7.   Ibid.

CHAPTER

15
COORDINATION

Some of the disenchantment with aid is due to
the fact that it has been, at the same time, too
fragmented and too global: divided and aggregated
along the wrong lines. The fragmentation is the
result of the numerous bilateral donors' aid programs,
each inspired by its own complex blend of motives,
objectives, and criteria. In addition, there are
the specialized agencies of the United Nations, again
pursuing their own objectives and guarding jealously
their spheres of competence. At the receiving end,
sovereign national governments are usually accepted
as the ultimate authorities for aid requests, with
little regard to regional and subregional coordination.
There have been signs of a beginning of coordination
between donors, between specialized agencies, and
between recipients. Consortia and consultative groups
are examples of the former, and the UN regional commissions examples of the latter. Marshall Plan aid
and the Alliance for Progress were unilateral on the
donor's side but attempted regional coordination,
cooperation, and integration on the side of the
recipients. The regional development banks are
another illustration of a move toward limited super-
national groupings of the right kind.

Africa, more than most regions in need of a
regionally planned and executed program, has enjoyed
least the benefits of such a program. The aid effort

has reinforced the historical, geographical, and political fragmentation of the continent and the fluctuations of aid over time, its unreliability, and its volatility in response to political forces have aggravated the already difficult problems of coordination and forward planning.

The setting up of consortia and consultative groups by the World Bank and the DAC is one move in the right direction. These new forces provide a valuable means of combining desirable features of bilateral with those of multilateral financial assistance. They are, however, "only concerned to a very limited extent with technical assistance."* The recent preoccupation of certain consultative groups (for Tunisia and East Africa) with such areas as education and agriculture may foreshadow a move on the part of the consortia and consultative groups to extend their field of action.

"The work in the consortia and consultative groups clearly demonstrates the advantages of a co-ordinated approach under the sponsorship of an international institution."** However, this kind of operation is not without its difficulties. Again, "In particular, the lack of any pledging or commitment by donors in the consultative groups put a considerable strain on the active co-operation of the beneficiary country."***

Between 1964 and 1966 countries that are members of consortia and consultative groups on the average received 37 percent of net official disbursement of the DAC countries. However, the setting up of consortia or consultative groups for particular developing countries has not, as might have been supposed, so far had the effect of notably biasing aid distribution in their favor and evening out fluctuations. This can be seen from Table 27.

---

*OECD, 1968 Review.

**Ibid.

***OECD, 1967 Review.

The consortia arrangements seem to have been
rather more successful than the consultative groups.
Of the four consortia countries, only Turkey shows a
reduced share and lower per capita receipts in 1966
as compared with the year of inception. The only
cases in which there seems to have been a definite
tendency for their percentage of total official aid
receipts to increase subsequent to the establishment
of a coordinating organization are those of the two
IBRD consortia countries, India and Pakistan (the
fall in 1966 is partly attributable to the border
war between the two countries in late 1965), and
Nigeria among the consultative group countries.

Eight of the fourteen consortia and consultative
group countries (accounting for more than half of
the total population in this group) had aid receipts
per head in 1966 below the average for all LDCs.
The rise in their aid receipts per head over the period
merely reflects the fact that the volume of total
aid, as well as aid for these countries, has on average
risen faster than their populations. More recently
the per capita aid receipts of consortia and consultative group countries as a group have been declining--
from the annual average of $3.21 over the period
1964-65 to $3.00 over the years 1966-68, whereas aid
receipts per head of all developing countries as a
group show a rise. (See Table 28.) Seven of the
fifteen countries saw lower annual average per capita
receipts in the later period.

The volume of net official assistance to two of
the three African consultative group countries has
fluctuated considerably, and the receipts of Sudan
and Tunisia were in fact lower in 1966 than in 1963
(the year of their inception); they show a rise in
1967 but Sudan's receipts still remain below the
1963 level, as can be seen from Table 29.

The arrangements for Nigeria show much more
satisfactory results, the volume of aid having increased seven times over the period 1963-67. In
1967, two further consultative groups were set up:
Morocco and East Africa. It is too early yet to
make an evaluation of their work. It can, however,

TABLE 27

Consortia and Consultative Groups: Shares of Countries in Net Total Official Aid Receipts and per Capita Aid Receipts, 1960-66

	Date of Inception	Percentage of Total Official Disbursement							Per Capita Aid Receipts (U.S. $)						
		1960	1961	1962	1963	1964	1965	1966	1960	1961	1962	1963	1964	1965	1966
Consortia															
India	1958	17.2	12.2	12.6	15.5	19.5	19.4	17.8	1.8	1.5	1.6	2.1	2.5	2.6	2.5
Pakistan	1960	5.8	4.9	6.8	8.0	8.4	7.7	6.0	2.6	2.6	3.7	4.6	4.6	4.5	5.5
Turkey	1962	3.0	3.4	3.9	3.5	2.6	2.8	2.9	4.9	6.6	7.8	7.3	5.2	5.9	6.2
Greece	1962	1.0	1.3	0.6	0.6	0.7	0.7	0.6	5.4	8.3	4.1	4.3	5.1	5.7	4.8
Consultative Groups															
Nigeria	1962	0.8	0.6	0.5	0.3	0.9	1.4	1.3	1.1	0.9	0.8	0.4	1.3	2.3	2.3
Colombia	1963		1.2	1.3	1.7	1.7	0.9	1.4	-0.4	4.1	4.5	6.3	5.9	3.4	5.5
Sudan	1963	0.7	0.4	0.4	0.3	0.4	0.5	0.2	2.8	1.9	1.7	1.5	1.9	2.2	1.2
Tunisia	1963	1.1	1.7	1.2	1.4	1.2	1.4	1.0	13.3	23.5	17.1	20.2	16.8	20.9	16.0
Ecuador	1964	0.3	0.3	0.3	0.3	0.3	0.3	0.4	3.5	3.6	3.9	3.0	2.4	3.0	5.2
Thailand	1965	1.1	0.7	0.9	0.7	0.5	0.7	0.8	1.9	1.4	1.9	1.5	1.1	1.5	1.7
Malaysia	1965	0.3	0.4	0.5	0.2	0.3	0.5	0.7	1.8	2.4	3.6	1.5	1.8	3.7	5.1
Ceylon	1965	0.3	0.3	0.3	0.2	0.2	0.2	0.5	1.4	1.4	1.7	1.4	1.1	1.4	2.7
Peru	1966	-0.2	-0.3	0.3	0.4	0.7	1.1	1.0	-1.0	-1.4	1.5	2.0	3.6	6.0	5.4
Korea (South)	1966	5.5	4.2	4.1	4.2	2.8	3.3	3.0	10.1	9.0	9.0	9.7	6.2	7.8	7.3
Average All LDCs									3.2	3.8	3.9	4.1	4.0	4.2	4.1

Note: In 1967 two further consultative groups were set up in Africa: Morocco and East Africa (comprising Kenya, Uganda, and Tanzania).
The Underlined figures show the year when disbursements resulting from the consortium or consultative group started.

Source: OECD, 1968 Review, p. 144.

TABLE 28

Consortia and Consultative Groups: Total Net Official
Aid Receipts, per Capita, as a Percentage
of Imports and of GDP, 1960-69

| | Annual Average per Capita Receipts | | | | | | Total Official Aid as a Percentage of 1967 Imports of Goods and Services (annual average 1967-69) | 1968 GNP (percent) |
| | Bilateral | | Multilateral | | Total | | | |
	1960-66	1967-69	1960-66	1967-69	1960-66	1967-69		
Consortia and Consultative Groups	2.51	2.61	0.26	0.45	2.77	3.06	21.15	3.94
India	1.90	1.76	0.20	0.27	2.10	2.03	39.45	2.42
Pakistan	3.47	2.99	0.29	0.75	3.76	3.74	35.03	3.09
Turkey	6.18	4.90	0.12	1.59	6.30	6.48	27.25	1.87
Greece	4.71	4.27	0.76	0.68	5.47	4.95	3.35	0.58
Nigeria	0.76	1.14	0.17	0.48	0.93	1.62	12.11	1.69
Colombia	2.46	5.35	1.76	2.06	4.22	7.41	22.52	2.54
Sudan	1.21	0.67	0.68	0.67	1.89	1.34	6.83	1.28
Tunisia	17.60	19.21	0.73	2.27	18.33	21.48	38.34	9.55
Ecuador	2.97	3.86	0.94	0.89	3.91	4.75	11.51	1.84
Thailand	21.57	2.04	4.05	0.15	25.62	2.19	6.90	n.a.
Malaysia	2.04	3.64	0.80	1.24	2.84	4.88	4.13	1.51
Ceylon	1.36	3.83	0.27	0.06	1.61	3.89	12.94	2.62
Peru	1.38	2.95	1.11	1.04	2.49	4.01	4.99	1.06
Korea (South)	8.31	10.14	0.10	0.19	8.41	10.33	29.58	5.49
Morocco	7.08	5.39	0.34	0.73	7.42	6.12	14.37	2.99
Indonesia	0.31	2.66	0.03	0.01	0.94	2.67	36.82	2.76
East Africa	3.99	2.79	0.24	0.89	4.23	3.67	16.72	4.67
Total Developing Countries	3.51	3.64	0.38	0.59	3.89	4.23	15.90*	2.12*

*Secretariat estimates, excluding a number of developing countries for which data are not available.

Source: OECD, Development Assistance Review, 1970.

TABLE 29

Receipts of Net Official Assistance by Sudan,
Tunisia, and Nigeria, 1963-67
(million $)

	1963	1964	1965	1966	1967
Nigeria	16.2	53.2	94.6	93.0	113.4
Tunisia	84.9	72.1	91.5	70.4	104.3
Sudan	19.6	24.9	30.2	17.1	18.9

Note: These are official bilateral flows
(disbursements) from OECD/DAC countries and multilateral flows, net of amortization.

Source: OECD, Geographical Distribution of
Financial Flows to Less Developed Countries,
1960-64, 1965, 1966-67.

be said that the World Bank arrangement for East
Africa is of great significance because it aims at
subregional cooperation and is an attempt at financing
multinational projects.

Thus the evidence on the effectiveness of these
arrangements is equivocal. It remains true that it
would be useful to strengthen them, both directly
and indirectly by increased coordination all round
and a streamlining of the aid-giving machinery. An
improved aid-giving machinery is of particular importance for Africa as the region with special needs
which has particularly suffered from the trends out-
lined above.

One move in this direction, which could be of
considerable benefit to the African countries, would
be greater standardization of the criteria for project
financing. Different donors use different standards,
and this increases the difficulties involved in project

preparation, making the exercise more costly and
further straining the limited expertise available
to the African countries.

In fact, as we have seen, Africa needs above
all help in the preparation, execution, and management
of projects. Inability to prepare more and better
feasibility studies and to implement them has inhibited
aid to Africa and led to a systematic underestimation
of Africa's absorptive capacity.

Among the main directions of reform are the
following:

1.   Inclusion of Soviet donors in cooperating
machinery; the joint concern is development, and
coordination within this over-riding aim should be
possible.

2.   Commitment several years ahead, thus guar-
anteeing regularity.

3.   Encouragement of regional and subregional
development, which transcends national boundaries
and follows economic and ecological lines, and
provision of aid to (a) promote closer integration
and (b) compensate the losers from integration where
such compensation is required or desirable.

4.   Testing of all forms of financial and technical assistance by the criterion of whether they
contribute to a fuller mobilization of indigenous
resources. Larger contributions toward local costs,
so as to avoid biases toward capital intensity and
import intensity, technical assistance aiming at
using indigenous facilities and training local coun-
terparts, and enterprises that transfer ownership
and management are illustrations of this principle.

To all these priority objectives a soft-loan
multilateral African Development Fund could make a
crucial contribution.

ABOUT THE AUTHOR

PAUL STREETEN is Warden of Queen Elizabeth House, Director of the Institute of Commonwealth Studies, and Fellow of Balliol College, Oxford. He was Professor of Economics at the University of Sussex, Fellow of the Institute of Development Studies (1964-66), and Deputy Director-General of Economic Planning at the Ministry of Overseas Development (1966-68).

Mr. Streeten was a Rockefeller Fellow in the USA, Research Fellow at the Johns Hopkins University, Baltimore, and Fellow at the Center for Advanced Studies, Wesleyan University, Connecticut. He is a member of the UK National Commission of UNESCO, of the Governing Body of the Institute of Development Studies and of the Board of the Commonwealth Development Corporation. He has lectured in Japan, Trinidad, Argentina, Chile, Brazil, India, Pakistan, the Philippines, Ceylon, in several African countries and in most countries on the Continent of Europe. He has worked for international organizations and many developing countries.

Mr. Streeten holds an M.A. from the University of Aberdeen and from the University of Oxford, where he was a Scholar of Balliol College.